PRESENT LIKE A PRO

PRESENT LIKE A PRO

The Field Guide to Mastering the Art of Business, Professional, and Public Speaking

CYNDI MAXEY, CSP, and KEVIN E. O'CONNOR, CSP

St. Martin's Griffin
New York

www.stmartins.com

Design by Level C

LIBRARY OF CONGRESS CATALOGING-IN-PUBLICATION DATA

Maxey, Cyndi.
    Present like a pro : a field guide to mastering the art of business, professional, and public speaking / by Cyndi Maxey and Kevin E. O'Connor.
        p. cm.
    ISBN-13: 978-0-312-34773-4
    ISBN-10: 0-312-34773-1
    1. Public speaking. I. O'Connor, Kevin E. II. Title.

PN4129.15.M368 2006
808.5'1—dc22

                                                                2006040810

D   10

To Randy Wonzong, my first speech coach (Woodruff High School, Peoria, Illinois), who inspired a lifelong love for oral interpretation and public speaking.

—Cyndi Maxey

For Tim McNamara, who listened, believed, and encouraged . . . and still does!

—Kevin E. O'Connor

Advice to Preachers:

You've got to read yourself full,
think yourself ready,
pray yourself hot,
and let yourself go!

—Anonymous

Contents

Acknowledgments   xiii
Introduction   1

Part I   Love the Language   7

1   Aristotle Knew the Basics   9
2   Master the Vocabulary of the Customer   13
3   Turn Your Expertise into a Speech   16
4   Be Creative with Word Color   20
5   Use Writers' Tricks to Unify and Emphasize   26
6   Language Is Your Best Tool   31
7   Bring Out the Interpreter in You   36
8   Say it Differently   42

Part II   Prepare Like Crazy   47

9   Practice Is the First Priority   49
10   Begin So You Can Practice   54
11   Tape and Time Yourself   57
12   Know the First Four Minutes Cold   60
13   Give Yourself Think Time   65
14   Find Out What Happened Last Time   69
15   Set Yourself Up for Success   72

Part III   Respect the Client   77

16   Know Who the Real Client Is   79
17   Know What the Meeting Planner *Really* Wants   81

18   Know What the Audience Needs   85
19   Know What to Use and What to Lose   88
20   Be an Expert on the Culture   92
21   Know What Works with This Client   95

Part IV   Break the Rules   99

22   You Don't Have to Be Perfect   101
23   It's OK to Surprise Your Audience   106
24   Decide on Your Notes Policy   110
25   Begin Unexpectedly—Involve Your
      Audience!   113
26   End Unexpectedly   116
27   Face a Trend with an Antitrend   119

Part V   Create a Connection   123

28   Start with the First Step   125
29   Try a Three-Part Warm-up   127
30   Connect with a Grieving Audience   130
31   Connect via Stories and More   134
32   No Joke! Know the Risks   138
33   Practice Consistent Eye Contact   142
34   Use Your Introduction to Connect   144
35   Connect with Visual Simplicity   147
36   Connect with Visual Innovation   151

Part VI   Adapt to the Moment   155

37   When "Dr. Evil" Shows Up, Be Ready   157
38   When Your Presenter Doesn't Show, You Can
      Still Shine   160
39   Don't Let Murphy's Law Surprise You   163
40   When Asked to Edit, Be Prepared   167
41   When Asked for Your Opinion, Listen First   170

42   Beware of the Two-Year-Old in You   174
43   Inquire, Observe, and Learn   177
44   It's the Norm, Not the Exception   181

Part VII Propel the Image   183

45   Look Like You Mean It   185
46   Sound Like You Mean It   189
47   Don't Fall into the Apology Trap   192
48   Become One with Your Microphone   196
49   You Own the Power of Performance   199
50   Discover and Deliver Your Strengths   203

Part VIII Master Interaction   207

51   Walk a Fine Line When Facilitating   209
52   Always Remember: It's About Them   211
53   Become "Learner-Centric"   215
54   Technical Experts Are People Too   219
55   Be Prepared with Questions   223
56   Become a Master Teacher   227
57   Know the Nuances of Learners' Needs
     and Wants   230

Part IX Follow Up for More   233

58   Build Upon the Audience Perception
     of Your Expertise Before, During,
     and After Your Speech   235
59   The Eyes of the Audience Will Help You
     Follow Up   237
60   Ask for the Right Kinds of Information   240
61   Get Immediate Feedback   243
62   Determine the Next Step   247

Part X   Never Give Up   249

63   Every Presentation Counts—Every Time   251
64   Every Presentation Is Different Even When
     It Is the Same   255
65   When You're Being Coached, Listen
     and Respond Carefully!   257
66   Step Up to the Retreat-Planning Challenge!   260
67   Go Forward with Follow-up   265
68   When You Are Asked, Always Do More   268
69   Final Thoughts from Your Biggest Fans   272

Acknowledgments

The authors gratefully acknowledge all the friends and colleagues in work and life who made this book possible.

Thank you to our New York agent, Jay Poynor, whom we cherish seeing, planning and laughing with every chance we get.

Thank you to professional speakers and authors Tony Alessandra, Diane Booher, Les Brown, Roger Dawson, and Nido Qubein for their kind and trusting endorsement of our work.

Thank you to contributors and inspirers Jerilyn Willin, Jim Meisenheimer, Don Plass, Kathy Passanisi, Cheryl Perlitz, Brian Palmer, John Grobe, Tom and Jane Sweeney, the Walker family, Leslie Wilson, Bill Brooks, Caryn Amster, Pat Ewert, Molly Zimmer, Ilie Singeorzan, Steve Zagata, Rich "Cosmo" Costello, Mark Partridge, Rita Emmett, Brian Becker, Debra Bachman-Zabloudil, and Barry Lyerly for allowing us to use their stories and wise comments.

A special thank you to our dynamic editor at St. Martin's Press, Ethan Friedman, for his energy, savvy, and focus, which only a really, really skilled editor can bring to a project. Thank you also to Jenness Crawford for her responsiveness and talent. And to our first editor, Julie Kaiser, who helped make our ideas come alive on paper.

Thanks to our families, especially Cyndi's dad, Ken Adcock, and Rob, Ryan, and Phelan Maxey, for their interest, love and support.

Also to Rita, Lanty, and Corbb O'Connor for their continuing encouragement; and to Betty Anne Cyr for her early and detailed work on this manuscript.

And last, thank you to the National Speakers Association, the unique international organization of professional speakers that brought us together in the first place.

Introduction

- "I am a terrible presenter."
- "The audience looked so bored!"
- "I didn't know how to answer that question; who would have thought he would ask that?"
- "I'm not that funny."
- "I'm not supposed to memorize my speech? So what will I say?"
- "Maybe you could present instead of me."
- "As part of your interview for this job, we'd just like you to give us a short presentation."
- "I hate presenting!"

Join a conversation with anyone who has to present to a group, emcee an awards ceremony, or simply toast the bride, and you will hear protests laced with procrastination, fear, and dread. In spite of living in an increasingly educated, technologically savvy, and media-aware society, most people still hate to prepare and deliver a presentation.

Why is giving a successful presentation such a challenge? What will empower you to rise to that challenge? The odds appear to work against you. When you present to a group, there is only one shot to impress the audience, leave a lasting impression, and earn the honor to be invited to speak again. If you speak infrequently, this can be a daunting experience. Professional speakers, on the other hand, typically speak from fifty to a hundred fifty times a year; that's one to three times a week! Even though you don't experience that much "air time," those times you do speak in front of a group are very important.

An employee we coached once asked: "Well, they surely aren't going to make personnel decisions on my presentation tomorrow ... are they?" Our answer to him and to you? *"Yes!* They *always* make personnel decisions when you stand up to speak!" Your presentation is a profile of you!

View each speaking opportunity as a "pro-stretch" and use the ideas in these pages to quickly and confidently learn and implement the skills and techniques of the professionals. Many presenters mistakenly believe that once they "get this over with" they will be in the clear—that the presentation is a necessary evil. What they don't understand is that their presentations are a stage for their careers. Like it or not, relaxed and confident presenters are seen as more competent, more skilled, and having more promise than their counterparts who are equally skilled and equally bright. When you present well, you become more believable, more convincing, and perceived as a better employee than someone who cannot do as well in front of an audience.

The good news is you can give great presentations, despite reluctance, low presentation self-esteem, a busy schedule, and a past history of fear or intimidation. You can learn skills that the pros use. How? Think of it this way: You may not be Tiger Woods, but you can learn to play a good game of golf. You may not be a translator for the United Nations, but you can learn enough Spanish or French to enjoy a vacation. In the same way, you can learn to become a more confident presenter.

In this book, you will not only learn the pros' secrets, but you will also have a field guide to take along and consult before the presentation. Your field guide is organized in sections that address your most immediate needs—as you determine them. You may start in the middle, the end, or with Aristotle—at the very beginning! It's up to you. You will discover the added benefits of a personal coach who speaks to you in every chapter. We will immerse you in time-tested tips gathered in "From the Pros" and real-life learning from people just like you in "From the Ranks." Throughout, we'll answer your "burning questions" (those questions at the top of your priority need-to-know list) and supply you with easy ways to remember things in "Three Ways to . . ." summaries. Let this book give you a "pro-stretch" warm-up on the invigorating road to speaker success. Here are three things you can do to prepare:

- **Be different.** Create what people don't anticipate. Start with a story they'd never expect. Consider something other than computer visuals to prove a point. Do innovative research—speak to everyone's administrative assistant before writing the speech. Give the entire speech on a flip chart. Practice in a room without lights! Draw on your natural style. You know what's interesting about you, your best stories, how you make kids laugh, and what you're inherently passionate about. Look within and find a difference that will make you memorable.

- **Be deliberate.** Approach this skill in a detailed and devoted way using this book as a field guide. Use it, read and reread chapters, consult this guide moments prior to the presentation, and use it to evaluate what went right and what to improve next time. Like any good field guide, this one should not stay on the shelf, but find a home in your briefcase.

- **Be determined.** Realize that while presenting may be occasional, real success is never an occasional pursuit. This book, while ever encouraging and positive, does not attempt to make great presentations easy: It only makes them attainable. Our goal is for you to systematically work on your needed skills while at the same time polishing existing ones.

Real growth is based on "stretch"—the ability to go
beyond what is comfortable and secure. To "pro-stretch"
is to add to your behavioral résumé the skills that
others see and judge.

HOW TO READ THIS BOOK

This Book Is Different

It is laid out in sections that are designed to set *you personally* up for *success* reaching your *particular* speaking goal. To get a feel for the topics covered in each section, we suggest that you first skim through the table of contents, noting the theme of each mini-chapter and the questions it answers. Do they coincide with your immediate concerns and questions? Then, select the section that speaks to you. Here are some ideas:

Ministers, Managers, and Other Inspirers

The first section, "Aristotle Knew the Basics," is definitely for you. Maximize your natural vocal and poetic abilities as well as your storytelling savvy here. In chapter 4, learn to be creative with word color; in chapters 5 and 6, get an overview of writers' tricks and using language. Chapter 8 encourages you to say it differently than everyone else.

Nervous Bridegrooms and Partners, Anxious Speakers

Reading part II, "Prepare Like Crazy," will calm your nerves and teach you the practicalities of giving a presentation—like practicing! Chapters 10 and 11 suggest lots of practice ideas, including timing and taping yourself. Chapter 14 stresses the importance of finding out what happened before and chapter 15 is on setting yourself up for success in front of the family or the boss. If you're asked to give a eulogy, you'll find good ideas in chapter 30 on how to connect with a grieving audience.

Salespeople

If you're a salesperson looking to upgrade your pitch, you may want to start with part III, "Respect the Client," which emphasizes client culture and audience needs. Chapter 16 lets you know who the real client is; chapters 17, 18, 20, and 21 encourage you to do lots of client research so you're an expert on the client's world.

Managers

If you're a new manager looking to make a great first impression with your first team meeting, you might start with the "Create a Connection" section, which lists quick and clever ways to start differently and engage the audience. Chapters 28, 29, and 34 focus on connection in the opening, using three different techniques. If you've been around awhile and would like to surprise your team with something new, read part IV, "Break the Rules." Chapter 23 will assure you it's OK to surprise them.

Team Leaders

If you have to give a ten-minute update in front of your peers, read chapters 23 and 25 in the "Break the Rules" section. And don't forget to "Propel the Image" as part VII reminds you, especially with chapters 45 and 46. If you're interrupted, you can learn to "Adapt to the Moment," as part VI describes in chapters 37 and 40.

Professional and Experienced Speakers

For those of you who are up in front frequently, there are great tips in part VI, "Adapt to the Moment," and part IX, "Follow up for More," which will allow you to stand out from the crowd even more than you already do. You will be able to handle unforeseen difficulties even more smoothly. Take a look at chapters 37 and 39 for ideas on troubleshooting the unexpected. If you have to meet with the meeting planner before your talk, learn how to ask the right questions in part III, "Respect the Client."

Best Men (or Women)

If you're preparing your wedding toast, and have never—ever—used a microphone, you will find confidence-building tips in part VII, "Propel the Image." Chapters 46 and 48, specifically, show you how.

Trainers and Facilitators

You may be looking to brush up your techniques when the group is talking and you're not! Read part VIII, "Master Interaction," first. Chapters 51, 52, and 53 can help you focus on the learner. If you need special help with technical experts, read chapter 54.

Occasional Presenters

If you have to address your fellow Rotarians, Jaycees, Kiwanis, or Lions, start with "Prepare Like Crazy" and set yourself for success. Or, the conclusion, "Never Give Up," may be where you want to start! Everyone needs a coach, an internal willpower, and a way to overcome mistakes. Get inspired by beginning with the end.

You—Our Reader—Are Different, Too!

Once you complete a section, process it a bit in your mind. Then do something. Take action. Write something. Say something out loud. Ask a friend or coworker. E-mail an idea. Edit an old one. Perhaps even give a presentation. Then read another section, and another . . . and so on. When you finish the book, you'll find your burning questions answered in many areas where presenters of all kinds have experienced challenges and blocks. But you won't be blocked again. You'll present with pizzazz.

THREE WAYS TO READ THIS BOOK

- Skim through the first time and read whatever catches your fancy.

- Keep this book on your desk or in your car. Right before your next presentation, read two or three chapters and notice the difference that makes in your speech.

- Buy a copy for your coach and work strategically together toward new goals.

Part I

Love the Language

1

Aristotle Knew the Basics

- **Power is in the character of the speaker.**
- **Power is in the speech itself.**
- **Power is in the mood of the audience.**

Why should you look forward to your next presentation? Because it's an absolutely irreplaceable experience! You get back much more than you give—every time you present.

First, giving a successful presentation is great for your psyche; you feel good when you do well. It even feels good when you try new things and not all go well.

Second, it is a practical way to move up in your organization or circle of friends and associates. If you are good at presenting, people automatically think you are good at everything you do because they see you as a courageous person with not only high self-esteem but also high "act-ability"—someone who does things. People give a lot of credence to a speaker; often it's simply because the speaker is up front and they are not! Standing up and speaking well are keys to your promotability quotient.

Third, you have personal power when you have command of an audience. To persuade a busy group of people to take notice of your message and to do something about it as a result ranks high on the scale of winning friends and influencing people.

The presenter's power is great. In fact, your ability to use that power well was first prescribed in an ancient art form perfected by the Greeks—the art of rhetoric. Some of the most well known philosophy comes from Aristotle (384–322 BC), who believed that people have a natural disposition for the truth and who called rhetoric "the ability to see the available means of persuasion" on the speaker's part.

The available means of persuasion for you are basically three elements: you, the talk, and the audience. That's it. Everything you do is a carefully concerted blend of these three. Giving a toast to the bride and groom? It's you, the toast, and the wedding guests. Addressing your new staff? It's you, your notes, and a group of people who are wondering about you. Selling a key account? It's you, your notes and visuals, and the three decision makers at the end of the boardroom table.

The balance of the three elements is key. Aristotle's view held that character of the speaker, the emotional state of the listener, and the argument itself (the talk) all combine to achieve the persuasion. He said the speaker has three powers: ethos, logos, and pathos. Ethos is the power of personal character. Logos is the power of proving a truth through logic. Pathos is the power to stir up emotions in the listener. The best presenters find a way to use all three powers in the right combination: who you are, what you say, and how you say it.

Your character is in your shared self. The best presenters communicate naturally as real people. They don't try to be someone they are not. One of our favorite professional speakers, a former penniless immigrant who is now a millionaire, is in demand today as a speaker because of the stories he tells and the many examples he gives of how he amassed his fortune. But he does it with little ego and lots of reverence for his friends, his beliefs, and his business relationships. All this is inherent in his character as he speaks. The audience believes him because of the power of his character.

COACH'S COMMENTS

Question: How can I communicate naturally when my natural self hates to speak to groups?

Your coach says: Most people do! Despite your dislike of speaking, one way to bring out your natural self is in the opening. You can do that by using an approach that nobody else would use and communicating it naturally because you have really, really practiced! The more you practice, the more natural you will be. It sounds odd, but it's true. When you think less about your words, you can think more about being yourself.

Your truth is in your argument and knowledge. How does a speaker find truth? Sometimes you may need to research and document to prove your points—in a sales presentation, for example. Other times you may not need intense research to support your thoughts. As long as you present evidence of the truth in the best way you know how, you demonstrate logos, or your reasoning. If you don't present with reason, the audience will quickly dismiss you as unqualified to speak. A minister or priest speaks with the evidence of the Bible. A professor brings research and case studies. An introducer brings knowledge of the speaker being introduced. Any talk, no matter how long, is truth telling. The more clarity to the truth you tell, the more convinced your audience is of your message.

Your emotional appeal is in your audience's hearts and minds. Of the three powers, this is the least predictable. You can learn to share your character and select your arguments more readily than you can pick up on the nuances of an audience. How will they react? What will they feel? What will they think? This power is perfected only by practice and listening to feedback— over and over again. If you really listen, you'll realize that your audiences are talking to you all the time—before, during, and after your presentation.

The true pro becomes adept at continuously gathering this information . . . day after day, speech after speech. It's best to avoid attempting to speak to any audience without first meeting them. Perfect opportunities include: at the dinner the night before, at breakfast the day of your presentation, moments before you go on. Your best opportunity is to approach audience members with a smile and a handshake and even ask the audience for their "burning questions," questions that bring out what the audience

really wants to learn from your talk. All of these are vital methods
used by the most successful of presenters who never forget this
essential third element.

**A presentation is an exercise in
the acknowledgment of power.**

2

Master the Vocabulary of the Customer

- **Words convey understanding.**
- **Audiences want most to be understood.**
- **Your meeting planner is your secret guide to your audience.**

Whoever asked you to speak is your customer. Although the audience is the one you are speaking to and with, it is the meeting planner, the one who gets you to the audience, who is your primary customer. A meeting planner may be a sales manager, a supervisor, the communications director, your school principal, your alderman, a training director, a marketing leader, a project team leader, or the bride or groom.

This person is also your greatest ally in learning about the audience. Meeting planners know those you are speaking to, they know their needs, and they know one thing you may not know—the special vocabulary of the audience.

Nothing will hurt you more with an audience than not conveying to them that you understand their work or their situation. Words, special words, convey that better and faster than anything else. For example, in the military, the term "TDY" refers to "temporary duty elsewhere." If someone is TDY, then they are on a temporary assignment.

Kevin and Cyndi both speak frequently to physicians, although they are not doctors. Kevin often teaches for the military, although he has never been in the military. The first time Kevin spoke to a group of Air Force physicians, he remembered that someone had mentioned a late-night party the night before, and how the physicians might not be very "awake" when Kevin spoke to them the following morning. Kevin was beginning what would be a full day of presentations when an officer came into the room making a real commotion by tripping and spilling his coffee. The audience, of course, looked up and laughed. Kevin said, "It's OK, he was just TDY for a bit last night." He laughed, and so did they. At the end of the day, one of the doctors approached Kevin and said, "I wasn't sure you'd be any good, but when you said what you said about TDY this morning, I knew you knew us."

COACH'S COMMENTS

Question: My supervisor is always my meeting planner. She seems to think I should know everything about my audience and not bother her with questions. Any ideas?

Your coach says: Ultimately, if you look good, she looks good— so don't give up. Try subtle ways to get information. In an e-mail about a project, ask her for any statistics she may have that will help you. In a conversation about something else, add, "By the way, for Friday's meeting, do you have any idea if the new IT manager will be present?" You can also compliment her and then ask for information, like this: "You are so great with details. Would you mind copying me on the results you collected of the last customer survey? That would help my presentation a lot."

Every audience wants to be known. Use your meeting planner to find out what the code words are. Does this audience have customers or clients? Do they have staff, employees, associates, crew, or cast members? Find out what happened in the presentation just prior to yours (attend that presentation!) the day before, the week before. Be curious about their work, their jargon, and their major challenges.

Are they an organization, an agency, a corporation, or an association? When Cyndi first addressed government audiences, she learned to speak about the reporting structure differently;

government leadership positions are chiefs and directors, not vice presidents and managers. Government employees talk about service and productivity, not profit and loss.

Then, interlace this knowledge in your presentation. Resist the temptation to be patronizing: "I think firefighters are the finest people in the world." Likewise, resist the temptation to act like you are one of them: "Whenever one of us sells a kidney dialysis machine, we know how important it is for the patient." Don't try to deliver all of your research too obviously to them: "I asked your meeting planner about you and I learned that you . . ."

Interlacing your knowledge means you may or may not use the tidbits you have learned. Kevin didn't know he would use TDY, but he kept it handy. As far as he knows, it only made a difference to one doctor. But it was an important difference.

Utilize your meeting planner for insight on the words that will reach your audience.

FROM THE RANKS

"As a person who has worked with speakers for years, I am constantly amazed at how little homework they do on the audience they are going to be presenting before. I had an experience once where a very well regarded speaker got up in front of an audience full of health-care executives (the American College of Healthcare Executives) and had his entire talk gauged to physicians! He literally did not have a clue that he was talking to administrators. One quick trip to the Web site would have set him straight."

—Debra, meeting planner for a health-care association

3

Turn Your Expertise into a Speech

- **Your life and work experiences make you unique.**
- **Be more aware every day of everything you do.**
- **Write down ideas ASAP.**

A Texas community leader called a longtime friend, one of the only female ranch owners locally, to invite her to talk about her ranch experiences to a few people the community leader was having for lunch. The rancher accepted and wrote a short, casual speech. To her surprise, the "few people" turned out to be eighteen hundred people at a large hotel! She gave the speech to much laughter, and happily, the feedback taught her that people liked her stories. She decided she loved speaking, pursued the field, and is now a sought-after professional speaker.

You may not lead an exciting, celebrity-filled life on a ranch with cowboys, rodeos, and Argentine millionaire bull buyers. However, you certainly have lots of memorable life and work experiences. You can use them to increase your visibility and expertise. Here are some ways to get started.

List topics that are easy for you to talk about. What topics are easiest for you to discuss? Think of areas you enjoy discussing or those topics your business associates and friends frequently ask you about for advice. Think of the things you do every day and the lessons you've learned over time. For example, if you're in construction, you could talk about working with general contractors, teaming up with major architects, or growing your business. If you're a homemaker, you can discuss your quick recipe successes or what you've learned about raising teenagers. Remember, the key is to start with what's easy. Contrary to popular belief, it should be easy, not laborious, to write.

COACH'S COMMENTS

Your coach says: Turn your expertise into a speech. The critical thing is to both know what you are talking about (content) and thoughtfully consider how to speak about it (delivery). Delivery takes more time than content. Practice, speak with others, tape yourself, simplify, and then work on making your presentation understandable for your audience by finding the level that is comfortable for them. A medical speech for a Rotary group on heart disease will be different than the same content presented to fellow cardiac surgeons. Neither speech needs to be a complicated one, simply a focused one—focused on the recipients.

Collect stories. Collect stories and examples and write them down as soon as possible. You tell stories to your friends and associates every day and to your family at the end of the day. Record them. You can make notes in your personal data assistant, on a tape recorder, or in a notepad. They don't have to be major events—just authentic experiences from your life. For example, the next time you have a unique meeting, are inspired by a family member's comment, or have a memorable customer service experience, write it down.

Be aware of current events and trends. If you're not aware of what's going on around you, including what people read, watch on TV, listen to on the radio, or search for on the Web, you won't have a topic that grabs immediate attention. Publicists and journalists are masters at discovering developing trends. Professional speakers will tell you that one of their biggest responsibilities to audiences is to stay on the leading edge.

You can be a trend watcher, too. Watch what aging Baby Boomers are doing with their homes or businesses, how retailers are adapting to the growing Hispanic workforce, how the down-turn in the economy is affecting your consumers, and the continual renewal of the Internet.

Read respected publications that focus on national issues. Watch cable channels and TV programs geared to the age you want to address: high school teens, young professionals, or semi-retired older citizens, for example. Look in the "meetings and conventions" section of your newspaper to see how other speakers are positioning their topics for groups and associations. You can then align your topic to the trend. For example, you could discuss "how the economy affects today's long-term decisions," "how to network online with the real-estate community," or perhaps "how to manage a business in semi-retirement."

Develop three to eight key points about your selected topic. Listeners will forget most of what you will say, so don't make lists with dozens of ideas. Keep your points to a minimum. For example: "Four Keys to Success in Selling Services," "Eight Tune-up Tips for the New Hire," or "Six Scheduling Mistakes I'd Never Make Again." Then, you can insert your stories to illustrate the key points.

Consider a unique way to package the topic. If you're wondering about what makes you unique, go to a bookstore and see how authors repackage the same topic over and over. They just give it a new slant. Here are some possible examples of creative packaging for rather mundane topics:

- *What Firefighters Know About Your Building's Safety That You Don't*

- *Starting a Pool Cleaning Business: How to Take the Plunge*

- *Dollars and Sense: An Accountant's View on Low-Cost Maintenance*

- *RSVP: How to Respond to Your Customer*

Once you've prepared a talk, you'll be ready to accept the next time a community leader, career fair coordinator, or meeting planner calls. Most talks range from thirty minutes to one hour and include time for questions, which you'll enjoy answering because you'll know you've sparked an interest in your topic. Few things are more rewarding than an appreciative audience that has come to hear your unique perspective and expertise.

**Each person is an expert at something
and loves to talk about it.**

FROM THE RANKS

"Once, after a long, rather ordinary day, I arrived to pick up an order from our printer who promptly announced that I was the winning customer of the day and that my order was free. Happily surprised, I asked why I was selected. He replied: 'Oh, we pick one person every day and you're it.' I wrote down the story immediately. What a great example for my customer service team at work!"

—Connie, administrative assistant

4
Be Creative with Word Color

- **Words are powerful: They can help or they can hurt your presentation and your audience.**

- **Your audience will respond to you differently depending upon the words you choose.**

- **The color of your words is sometimes more important than the words themselves.**

How do you want to say it? How do you want to greet this audience? How do you want them to think of you after they leave and describe you and your talk to someone else?

Your word choice is critical when it comes to both impacting your audience in the moment and remaining in their memory after the presentation concludes. Do you want to say something is "bad" or that it was "unfortunate"? Is it really "depressing" or could it be "discouraging" or even better, "a bump in the road"? How will the audience feel if you speak of "firing" an employee rather than "letting him or her go," "helping the employee find a real vocation in life," or perhaps "structuring a dignified way to leave this job and find something else to contribute to more effectively"?

The "color" of your words is the punch they give the audience. In much the same way real color helps us distinguish what is important and critical, so too does the color of a word. Consider these word pairs. In each case, which stands out for you as more colorful?

Happy/exultant
Good/first-rate

Bright/luminous
Challenge/face up to
Discussion/debate
Dream/reverie
Great/absolute
Growing/on the rise

Overuse can take away the true color of a word and leave it stale, bland, and ordinary. Consider these corporate buzzwords, resounding too frequently at meetings everywhere. What do they really mean?

Best practice
Outside the box
With the game plan
Benchmark
Value-added
Movers and shakers
Big picture
Total quality
Proactive
In the loop
Out of the loop
Too much on my plate

Words are much more than "spin." Great presenters consciously choose their words to convey the right meaning at the right time to the right person. The presenter's first duty is always to think of the listener. What do I want the listener to understand? How can I say this so it will impact the listener's mind and clearly express my intentions?

None of us read minds. We don't ever know what is actually going on inside another's brain. However, although we cannot be mind readers, we can be mindful communicators. Mindful communicators are careful of one thing above all else: How is my message being received? They are less concerned with what they are saying compared to what is being heard. Certainly, they need to attend to their message, making it clear and "listen-able." But when it comes to communication, the best communicators care more about the receiver of their message.

It makes sense when you consider how all of communication is really nothing more than what two people understand words to mean. Imagine beginning with, "Good morning, and how is everyone doing today?" These are simple words, but by the inflection in your voice you can be welcoming or sarcastic, funny or cute, hurtful or helpful. By the nonverbal cues you use or the ones you are unaware of, you can cut your message short and inspire resentment or even anger in the listener.

When it comes to word color, a presenter's understanding of the chosen words will further the message with the receiver. Today's audiences are savvy enough to know if they're hearing something redundant, manipulative, or borrowed from yesterday's news.

COACH'S COMMENTS

Your coach says: Rehearse the words you will use. Don't rely on the spontaneous moment. Select. Rehearse. And then do one more thing. Use these words in your casual conversation with others and see how they work. Comedians always try out their material informally before they ever hit the stage. Do the same.

Question: But I just present weekly accounting reports for the managers' meeting. Do I really have to worry about word color?

Your coach says: Words add life to your report. They take you from the mundane to the memorable, even when giving an accounting report. You will gain attention much more with "I literally jumped for joy when I saw these numbers—we've never been this far ahead of budget this early in the year!" than you will with "Here are the income/expense figures from the week of March ninth." Most people find financial reports and other technical topics interesting but dry, so delight the audience with words.

Word color is a skill you can learn and use regularly. Here's how. First, listen to yourself. Professional speakers actually record themselves on audio or video and then listen intently to what they really said. This is a very painful process! Like an actor watching his or her own film, you tend to see the flaws, the mistakes, and the miscues—supposedly what you need to pay attention to if you are going to get better. But contrary to popular wisdom, it is difficult to improve by focusing on mistakes. Don't do it!

Like a small child learning to walk, you only progress when you focus on the next right step that gets you to your goal. That's why it's often helpful to work with a trusted coach, adviser, or colleague who's skilled at pointing out your strengths. You may need to hear someone say, "Your voice is so smooth . . . so mellow . . . it just needs a little variety." Or, "I like the way you keep referring to the winning sales team. What's another way you could emphasize this?"

Second, listen to those who talk about your presentation afterward. Audiences are a wonderful and abundant resource—if only we were willing to listen. They come up to us and literally tell us what we said from their own unique point of view. Sometimes it is not even what we really said!

Kevin had an occasion where a good friend went on and on about a story he had told the day before in a presentation. As Kevin politely nodded, she went on retelling his story, but her version had an entirely different point and punch line! Kevin had the presence of mind to ask a question before he thought about trying to correct her: "What did that story mean to you?" he asked. She then shared her own personal story about how his remarks conveyed the importance of courage at a time when she was struggling with her son's addiction to alcohol. She did what many in your audiences will do—she took his story, combined it with her story, and cemented the result in her own real-life experience.

It is critical to understand that listeners do this. Otherwise we will try to cajole, convince, out-argue, and debate—all forceful things that use our words with little to show for them. Make it a habit to ask every single audience member who approaches you after the talk what stood out for him or her. You will learn immediately what is most meaningful. After a civic luncheon keynote,

Cyndi asked several audience members what they found most memorable, and she was surprised to find that many of them described how they felt afterward. They said things like, "I was inspired," or "It was just so nice to hear the stories . . . made me feel less alone." Cyndi knew that while she had appealed to emotions, perhaps her stories weren't making the solid content points she had intended.

Your audience knows what you said better than you do!

Third, listen to others as they present, no matter what setting. Whether you are one of five hundred or a thousand or one of four in attendance at a church meeting, watch others' word usage. Which words impact you? Which words help you listen and imagine? How does the speaker compel you to listen?

Some speakers use specific techniques to capture our interest. They raise the level of the microphone and speak louder—and the audience thinks they know more! Some engage in highly emotional, sometimes predictable stories of heroism or victory or patriotism in order to move the audience. Some tell jokes or share personal stories to get a laugh and warm the audience to them and their message. Some speak with great authority, so that the audience thinks that they must know what they are talking about! Remember, Hitler was a terrific, mesmerizing speaker—and he used each of these techniques, except the humor.

Your words can help or hurt. You as the presenter have enormous power for good or ill. Be especially vigilant with words related to gender or ethnic background. A "mailman" is now a "letter carrier." The word "actor" can encompass both men and women. Check to see if a group prefers to be called African-American, black, minority, Hispanic, Asian, pan-Asian, Nordic, Germanic, Indian, American, Native American, Northern, or Southern, for example. The wise speaker communicates with an educated, careful choice of any word that may inhibit, hurt, or limit the acceptability of his or her talk.

Truly significant speakers go beyond technique and aim for substance. They clearly know what they are going to say, they have an inner mission to say it, and they rely on what is known as "conversation" in order to say it. Even when they are the only speaker, these presenters converse with an audience as if they were speaking one-on-one.

You can do this, also. When you listen to yourself, to your listeners, and to your presenters, you can sensitize yourself to using words for the benefit of the listener. And you can color their world in the process.

> **Contrary to popular wisdom, you don't improve by focusing on your mistakes—instead focus on those times when you've really connected with your listener. That's when you're doing something right!**

THREE WAYS TO TELL YOU'RE BORING THE AUDIENCE:

- **They glance at their watches.** Remember, interested audience members are not watching the time . . . unless you are!

- **They look ahead in the handouts.** This is not always a bad sign, but it might be good to "jump ahead" when they do and keep moving unexpectedly through your handout so that they "have" to listen to you. Whatever you do in this circumstance, don't be too predictable, even if your handout is.

- **They sneak looks at the silent messages on their cell phones.** One way to take care of this is in advance—ask for the meeting to be "technology-free," then ignore those who don't, unless they open their computer—then quietly remind them.

5

Use Writers' Tricks to Unify and Emphasize

- **The speaker can learn much from the writer.**
- **Writers are master thought organizers.**
- **Writers are master word users.**
- **The editor makes the writer look good.**

Neither of us has a degree in writing. Cyndi has an English minor and we both have taught English. But neither of us had any idea how much writing we would do in conjunction with our speaking careers, and for that matter, in conjunction with life! For speakers, writing is the basic building block for success. Without a well-designed talk, it's very difficult to communicate the message you want to send and it is nearly impossible to present like a pro.

Give your mind a place to start. If you're like most presenters, one of the hardest things to do is to get started; your mind is unfocused and the blank computer screen stares back with nothing to say. Yet, if you talk to writers, they will tell you their writing rarely starts from nothing. That's because most writers are continually thinking about writing, making mental notes about things, and formulating ideas that eventually become plots or themes. They jot things down on napkins or notepads or matchbooks. They share their thoughts with whomever they are with at the moment; they collect quotes and excerpts to cite from others' work.

Imagine the busy mind of a columnist who must constantly collect data for a weekly column. That's the disciplined writer's mind—never lazy, rarely bored, and always searching. In short, writers give their minds a place to start by never shutting off anything that might be useful to them.

Like the writer, you can also discipline your thinking. As you learn more about what people will typically ask you to present, you can become a constant collector of ideas. These could be random thoughts, newspaper clippings, a funny line or two, a poem, even a picture that alerts your interest. Speeches that are well done and speakers who present like pros rarely do so without preparation; you just don't see them prepare. Their active mind always searches for how to make ideas form a line, a section, a speech, or a coaching phrase. Your job is to organize your own ideas so they will be available to you when you need them. File them in some way and keep them available for the future. Here are some ways to collect ideas:

- **When you're at a meeting, take notes not only on the presenter's content but also on the ideas the content elicits for you.** For example, in the weekly sales meeting, make a note of the quota for the month. Then jot some questions next to the data to provoke more thought: Why do we have quotas? How are salespeople really motivated? Where are my best customers coming from?

- **While listening to a sermon, write down anything that strikes you as meaningful to your life or work.** The pastor at Cyndi's church uses great quotes from the arts; listening for these keeps her attuned to the sermon!

- **Write down what children say immediately.** It's often very funny and unintentionally profound!

- **Find lessons in everyday things:** washing hands, walking a dog, waking up, brushing your teeth. Walking a dog teaches you the joys of fresh air and using your senses, something everyone can relate to.

- **Save newspaper headlines, especially funny ones, different ones, and those that relate to your specialty.** Make sure you make note of the paper and the date on the back of the clipping for future use.

- **Thoroughly read your organization's monthly newsletter and refer to peoples' accomplishments later.** One master speaker we know actually sends a short congratulatory note to every writer in his organization's magazine!

- **Keep ideas in a file to pull out the next time you develop a talk.** This way, you won't have to start with a blank slate.

Avoid the bullet point trap. When charged with writing a presentation to a group, many people sit down at their laptops, open up visuals like PowerPoint, and start making bullet points, hoping their muse will float in. This technique, while good for organizing and clarifying details, can actually inhibit your creativity, trapping you as a victim of technology. Try for a combination. Write a short outline on paper first, let your mind cite three key ideas you want to develop, and chances are the perfect example or story will come to mind.

Become a word enthusiast. Writers are word enthusiasts. An accountant for a large corporation who was asked to improve his communication skills worked hard to listen and learned to love language. He began to write down words that people he admired used frequently, and he also wrote down words that were overused. He realized that people at work often don't have the vocabulary to express themselves well, and he began a mission to improve his own vocabulary. Speakers should use the thesaurus and dictionary tools frequently. They are a part of most word processing software and take only a few seconds to use.

Repeat key ideas for emphasis. Your audience thinks much faster than you can talk. In that time gap, they will daydream, lose interest, worry, plan their grocery lists, and meander mentally. If you repeat your key ideas and summarize frequently, the chances of your message sinking in will improve.

COACH'S COMMENTS

Your coach says: Summarize frequently with the use of "therefore . . ." or "let me review . . ." or "as an example . . ." Writers often do the same. They will tell stories or use examples to drive their point home and to create human interest. Whenever a speaker uses an example, you will notice that the audience has renewed attention. Watch your rabbi, priest, or minister's technique next service—they do it all the time! And it works like a charm.

On one occasion Cyndi coached a manager in pharmaceutical sales who was addressing his new regional team in person for the first time after several months of teleconferences. He wanted to show them he was experienced yet approachable. After some brainstorming, he remembered a story about his first experience with pharmaceutical sales representatives back when he was a young pharmacist. He had decided right then he wanted their job! He used the story in his opening with some humor. The rep's job often looks like a dream job from the outside. Then, in the closing, he tied the story back to the reality of the job, the hard work of the rep, and his admiration for his team.

Edit like a fairy godmother. How many words should you use? Cinderella's ugly stepsister tried to shove her foot in too small a shoe. The glass slipper was specifically and magically sized just right for its intended wearer. In the same way, size your talk just right for the audience. How long should your presentation be? A good rule of thumb: Think less rather than more— simple rather than complex. Most presentations are too long. Have you ever heard anyone say after a meeting, "Wow, I wish she had gone on longer!"? Probably not. Keep in mind, most of us benefit from working with an editor.

An editor reads with an eye to the overall intent of the work. He or she thinks: "Where is each sentence headed? Where are the unneeded angles and veers off the road? Does the writer ever self-aggrandize or condescend to the audience? Is there jargon that's difficult to understand?" While a professional editor is fast and perhaps a bit ruthless, most presenters don't have access to an editing pro. The next best thing? Ask a trusted colleague or partner to read or listen to your rough draft. It's well worth the time to test your words with one person before you face a group.

Writing and editing well are more than basic building blocks to speaking success: They can be keys to opening the mind of your audience.

6

Language Is Your Best Tool

- There is a great cultural divide between you and the audience even when you speak in your own "backyard."

- All language and meaning are relative to the listener—none of us sees life the way it really is; we only see what we see.

- No matter how precisely you say it, prepare to be misunderstood.

"What divides us may not be as important as what unites us"; however, speakers know there is a tremendous chasm between themselves and the audience. The old adage for speakers is "tell 'em what you are going to tell 'em, then tell 'em, then tell 'em what you've told 'em." This is hard-bought wisdom. Despite a common language, you will often speak to those who construct your message as you speak as if they spoke a different language.

Meaning is open to interpretation. You may think that because you're being precise, others will listen and understand your meaning. This is only partially true. Human beings interpret constantly and quite often from their own experience. When people are urged to "think out of the box," they are being asked to go beyond a familiar backyard of ideas and notions. This is no easy task. In addition to feeling respected and listened to, one of the great needs of humans is to be right, to feel correct, and to be on the right track. This is why people often listen with a third ear—the ear that listens for the familiar.

Everyone has a third ear. That is why language can be both your best and worst tool. It is, in fact, only one tool. You also have nonverbal communication, the synergy with the audience, and audiovisuals, but it is the language you speak and the language that the audience listens with that really conveys the message.

Therefore, language is your best tool only when you understand at a deep level that the audience quite possibly listens with a different ear. When you speak with a skeptical audience, you need to be aware of what they are skeptical about. If you talk about money, for example, try to understand what money means to your audience: security, stability, precision, future viability, personal income, power, prestige, or savings? When you deliver a eulogy, you must use the most appropriate words for greatest impact. Was the deceased called "Grandpa" or "Pa" or "Granddad" or "Buck" or "the Captain"? Get it wrong and you can imagine how you will be remembered when the day comes!

The mind needs repetition. Most audiences will forget much of what you said. They will even hear some of it completely wrong— very, very wrong. To combat this tendency, the best speakers repeat, illustrate, drive home, add some humor, purposely pause, and move around the stage to constantly reinforce their main message or the story they want the audience to leave with. Sometimes it is as simple as having the audience become more familiar with one another. Many professional motivational speakers now use audience warm-ups—brief ones—to help the audience discover commonalities. A few minutes spent on warm-ups better positions the audience for the next forty-five minutes of presentation. The speaker can then use the language that results from the warm-up exchange.

You can do this, too. Try asking your next audience to share one thing they loved about their job this past week or one thing they appreciate about their most difficult customers. You'll find you can build on their ideas and refer back to them as well as discover clues about how they use language.

Other times, repetition of the main theme is a key skill for the effective presenter. For example, the speaker introduces a seemingly simple concept like: "Customers need better service," or "We each see things differently," or "World-class service can take place in ordinary ways." This language needs to be reinforced several times to sink in with an audience, and the savvy presenter uses examples, illustrations, and testimonials to reinforce the theme.

COACH'S COMMENTS

Question: I give board reports for my church staff. They're very short—about five minutes—and while I want to be memorable, I'm fearful of repeating myself too much. Are there still ways to do this?

Your coach says: There are still ways to make a mark on the board's memory. You can be direct by saying something like: "There is only one word that describes the fundraiser this year—*energy*. There was energy in the planning, the volunteerism, and the troubleshooting when we sold too many tickets and had too few seats! I'd like to address that concern and plan ahead for next year so that energy can be put in a better direction." Also, even in five minutes, you can list three things and then repeat them at the end: "So, again, the three concerns for next year are advanced ticket sales, at-the-door pricing, and seating for walk-ins."

Understanding the theme is vital. This seems basic, but many times the theme is misinterpreted, assumed, or incorrect for the purpose at hand. One night, Kevin was ready to give an after-dinner presentation to a group of physicians and their spouses. The after-dinner slot is not the most enviable spot on the program! Drinks, food, late hour, and busy waitstaff all combined for the worst of venues. Kevin had prepared his presentation as he had been asked: ". . . something light and fun and under forty minutes." During the cocktail hour, two doctors casually mentioned to him how much they were looking forward to his presentation because, as one noted: ". . . These days at this conference are really about us coming together as a community more than any one thing we learn." Another mentioned that his experience with Kevin was that he ". . . didn't just talk at us, but involved us."

As he saw his forty-minute planned speech disappear before him,

Kevin decided to take a risk. He substituted his prepared remarks for an audience participation–filled, small-group discussion–oriented, very light program where the wine helped the laughs, the movement helped the sleepiness, and the interaction aided to the feel of community. You can imagine how grateful Kevin was to those physicians for their off-hand comments.

Everyone has an experience filter. When you speak to an audience, you compete with either a very tough enemy or a fantastic friend—the audience's experience filter. This filter remains constantly on. Audiences can listen much faster than we can talk. Remember the last time you were "listening" to a presentation? Weren't you also thinking about the evening activity, your children, or your grocery list, or even giving the speaker an on-the-spot silent evaluation? This is common and something every speaker must cooperate with rather than counteract.

Cooperate with this experience filter by getting to know the audience so well that you literally speak through the filter—use their words, their tone, their pace, and their issues. As members of the National Speakers Association, we often hear presenters speak about marketing and business planning. The ones who make the greatest impact and receive the best evaluations are the ones who've done their homework. We can tell because they quote statistics about us that are true; they are aware of the challenges of our business, and they are able to use terminology related to our field like "bureau bookings," "cancellation clauses," "learning tools and systems," and "platform mechanics."

You can do this, too, in a variety of ways. The way you open is perhaps most important. Don't start your talk with a typical comment about the weather or your bad flight into town. Instead, open with an Internet headline relevant to the group or a great anecdote about their manager.

When we say that the language is your best tool, we mean the language of the audience experience, not literally the spoken language and not only the words used. It is one thing to use medical jargon and quite another to understand the lived experience of a nurse or physician. One physician began a presentation with

"Remember that day, one of the first days, of residency when we had to . . ." Before he could complete his sentence, heads were nodding, faces smiling. He had them!

Kevin once opened a program with, "We now know for sure that the best way to retain nurses is through doctors." He then watched for who was nodding in agreement, and who was puzzled. Calling on a "head nodder," he asked, "What do I mean by that?" This particular doctor went on to make the best case for doctors treating nurses with the respect of a fellow professional. He had them!

You can achieve audience rapport in three ways: repetition, repetition, repetition. What is your main theme? Find at least three ways to illustrate it. What is the feeling you want your audience to have when you complete your presentation? Find three ways to feel that feeling yourself and to demonstrate it to them. And what do you want them to do after your talk? Make sure you tell them early, tell them often, and send them off after you told them one more time.

The next time you are listening to your favorite speaker, try to imagine his or her main point as a *National Enquirer* headline. *The National Enquirer*'s headlines always have an emotional tone to them and they are exciting to read, even if slightly modified from reality! Pay attention to how much repetition goes on in an effective speech. Even short church sermons of seven to ten minutes have an element that is repeated over and over in different ways.

Speakers don't repeat because audiences are stupid. Speakers repeat because they need to work through the filter of experience that so richly fills listeners' lives. When you learn to cooperate rather than compete with that inner voice of the audience, then you will be heard.

7

Bring Out the Interpreter in You

- **Your voice is an instrument.**
- **Words have color, emotion, and action.**
- **Your body clarifies and emphasizes your message.**
- **The eye of oral interpretation will give you 20/20 vision.**

When you deliver any kind of talk, you have a unique opportunity to become an interpreter . . . of your own language! Oral interpretation is actually an ancient art form that makes the written word come alive through the performer. In the Golden Age of Greece, interpreters were called rhapsodes. In Teutonic history, they were called bards, considered to be so important they sometimes actually decreed laws. In Wales, bards became too powerful and, at one point, were driven out. Historically, interpreting the written word with excellence has been a respected—even feared—skill!

Today, the ability to interpret with excellence adds meaning to your message. You've heard the adage, "It's not what you say. It's how you say it." It's true. How we say things makes a difference. From Adolph Hitler to your nightly newscasters, speakers attempt to influence not only through their ideas, but also how they say their ideas. Whether you are interpreting your own words or quoting someone else's, there are many ways to bring out the interpreter in you.

Play your voice like an instrument. It's an incredible thing—your voice. Did you know you have a capability for diction, enunciation, pitch, volume, tone, pause, emphasis, and tempo? There is no excuse for having a one-note presentation. Monotone speakers are either totally unaware of their natural capabilities or just plain lazy. When you are discussing important ideas like dazzling sales results, surprising research, key feedback, or disappointing attendance, you have a perfect opportunity to play your vocal instrument.

Your voice does not have to be naturally deep and beautiful; you can develop what you've been given. Words are very musical and your instrument is natural and uniquely yours. You, the speaker, can enroll your voice in the basics and work to become a great word interpreter. Pay attention to the voice of others. Who plays theirs well where you work? And what effect does it seem to have on you and on others? Your voice is more than a transmitter of words in the same way a radio is more than a series of electronic beeps.

Volume is the most important basic lesson for the voice. If your voice can't be heard, your message can't either. Volume begins with a deep breath supported by your diaphragm and aimed at the back of the room. Today it's often enhanced with a microphone, which needs to be tested just as your voice should be. Whether or not you're using a mike, ask a colleague or an early arriving audience member if you can be heard in the back of the room. Volume is power. You must be heard. The best speakers vary volume, speaking louder or softer to emphasize words accordingly.

The microphone is an instrument, too, and needs to be used skillfully. Not just an amplifier, the microphone is a tool that can help you become more effective. Stand-up comedians always use a handheld microphone. Why? Because they can "work the mike" by getting closer and farther away, using whispers, shouts, grunts, and groans in the same way an accordion player uses his or her whole body with the instrument. Professional speakers often use a lavalier microphone high up on their tie or blouse so that they can use their hands and arms freely for gestures that also convey feeling and emphasis.

Diction and enunciation both refer to the clarity with which you pronounce and articulate words. You must be understood not only for the listener's sake, but also for your own credibility. In conversation, people tend to run words together, as in "Whadjasay?" instead of "What did you say?" Often geographic regions are known for mispronunciations that never seem correct. In the southern Midwest, for example, the verb "wash" becomes "warsh" and "creek" becomes "crick." If you grow up in such a region, chances are you are not mispronouncing words when you are there, but you are seen as mispronouncing words in another region of the country. Most of the time, because they rarely get feedback, people don't realize how they sound.

Listen to national news reporters. These professionals strive to have an undetectable accent, generic enough so that we can all "hear" them according to our own native accent. Whether from the deep South, Brooklyn, the L.A. valley, or metropolitan Chicago, you each have an accent that tells where you are from. The secret is not to abandon your accent, but simply to be aware of when it is a problem for the audience.

To present like a pro, find out if you're easy to understand. Are your words clearly pronounced? Ask your friends and coworkers. Practice in the room you'll speak in. The biggest clue that you need to improve your diction is if people ask you to repeat things frequently. If you need to, work with a coach or repeat words on tape to improve. Even pros work on things like keeping the –*ing* endings or articulating end consonants on words like *end* or *then* or *forever*. The larger the group you address, the more precise your diction should be. If you have ever sung in a choir, the director probably told you to "open your mouth" as you sang. This is not done for volume, but for diction and precision. Forced to open your mouth, you become clearer—no matter where you were born!

COACH'S COMMENTS

Your coach says: Anybody can make a major mistake here by either mispronouncing the technical terms of the audience or by using them inappropriately. If you often speak to audiences who know much more than you do about your field, you can try what a speaker who speaks to physicians and pharmacists does! First, he circulates with the crowd or gets on the phone and asks individuals to "teach" him the term and the concept and (this is important) what benefit this term has for the audience. Then, he intentionally mispronounces the word (so he won't look like a "wannabe" know-it-all) and asks for audience help (they laugh), and then he gets serious by saying: "I have trouble saying 'pharmacoeconomics,' but I will tell you one thing, if you or I have trouble selling the concept to doctors, then you and I are up a creek without a prescription." When you know the benefit, the value, then the audience doesn't care if you are an expert in their work, they will see you are an expert in your stuff.

A lively, varied tempo and pitch will increase the chances of your message getting across because you'll never put your audiences to sleep this way! Vary your pitch by experimenting with the range of your voice. Count to ten without singing but by starting with your lower-register tones and ending with your highest-register tones and you'll be amazed at how low and high your range is. Vary your speed or rate with a pause. Pause is the true mark of the pro. To pause denotes confidence and skill. It also allows time for your audience to think. If you haven't used pause much as an interpretive tool, mark places in your notes where you want to pause or write the word "pause" on a note card near your laptop or notes to remind you.

Tone is the subtlest vocal tool you have, but a noticeable one nonetheless. If you have heard a piano or a guitar that's out of tune, you know how tone can affect the entire song. Likewise, your tone can impact your entire message. Decide on the overall tone you want to convey. Is it serious contemplation or lively creativity? Is it inspirational, friendly, upbeat, or challenging? One trick that pros use to maintain a friendly, light-hearted tone is to smile throughout—not a huge grin but a subtle upturning of the corners of the mouth. In sales research, it was discovered that when telemarketers spoke with a smile, customers felt they were friendlier. A smile will help you appear more approachable. Watch the news on TV. Unless it is a story of tragedy, most newscasters have a slight, warm smile throughout the broadcast.

Get your whole body involved. The professional oral interpreter typically sits on a stool with a script in front of him or her on an easel stand. The stage is simple with a black curtain in back and no set. Yet, for the audience, a whole world is created in the mind. The voice and the body of the interpreter combine to make the magic of nothing become something. If you want to achieve this effect, do the same thing the interpreter does even when sitting on the stool—get your body involved.

Create characters. You have a realm of choices. You can gesture, shrug, lift your eyebrows, pantomime an action, or turn your head to indicate talking to someone. A slight turn of your head left and right can easily and quickly establish that two people are speaking to one another. In oral interpretation, this is called "placement of characters" and it helps the audience understand the dialogue. You can use it to recount an exchange between two customers like this, "So one customer asked, 'How can I get an item exchanged on a day like today?' and the other said to her, 'I know what you mean. This is crazy.' "

Or, if you're toasting the bride and groom, you can use it in a dialogue like this, "So Joe said, 'I think, I mean I'm pretty sure, what I mean is, I want to marry you,' and Susie responded, 'My man of few words!' " A slight turn of the head establishes two characters in both scenarios. When you add some slight, subtle facial moves, him looking boyish, her looking confident and impatient, it works for the audience even better!

Tell the story. When you present, tell stories. Throughout the corporate world, presenters tell stories about the research, the data, the last meeting, the consumer's reaction, the annual conference, the sales strategy, the key customer's needs, or the new management team. At other gatherings, presenters tell stories about relatives, newborn babies, romantic love, children in need, and community history. We talk about stories in many different places in this book. This is because stories are so very important to the presenter. Stories are the most natural means you have to communicate. When you bring out the interpreter in you, you make the most of the story in your message.

For years, Porsche cars were sold with booklets of stories about how hardworking German automakers designed, fitted, and even painted all the parts. In fact, Porsche salespeople were taught to sell the car by walking around it and telling its stories. The technique was called "storytelling selling." The car was described as "a race car you can drive on the street." Prospects were encouraged to buy a car that "feels alive" and "talks to you."

It is always about the story. Look through your material and find the stories, not just sometimes, but every time you present. Next time you hear a sermon, watch the congregation as the pastor tells an illustrating story. They will rivet their eyes toward the pulpit—works each and every time, even with badly told stories. We all love stories!

Quote from others. Use other people's quotes and stories to emphasize and illustrate your own. Do them justice by using your voice and body to give color to the words. One of Cyndi's favorites when addressing stress and change is from Longfellow's "A Psalm of Life": "Let us, then, be up and doing,/With a heart for any fate;/Still achieving, still pursuing,/Learn to labor and to wait."

Longfellow provides a great opportunity to use emphasis, pause, inspirational tone, and even a gesture or two. Would that quote work well with a monotone? Try it for yourself, out loud. Monotone? Absolutely not!

The interpreter in you tells the story in a way nobody else can—with your voice, your body, and your selection of words.

8

Say It Differently

- **When you speak, don't just report; add value.**
- **When you add value, think of the receiver.**
- **When you think of the receiver, simplify.**

Although you will read books and reports to prepare for your talk, make sure you don't recite a book report. When you use others' quotes in your talk, make sure to be quotable yourself. A humorist speaker we know likes to say, "My favorite person to quote is me!" after he makes a particularly memorable quip. And when you must dispense information, take care not to dump data. Data dump is just lazy. You're more creative than that.

Whether or not you are an experienced speaker, the CEO or an intern, student or professor—when you get up to speak, make sure you think **value, receiver, simplicity.** There is no reason for a speaker not to consider these three things. Your audience can gather information from the Internet or the library or a phone call. They can tell themselves anything they want without fear of a poor evaluation—they are the receivers! Therefore, as a speaker you must consider their needs, preferences, and their ability to override what you say for what they believe. For speakers to worry only about the message and not the reception of the message is dangerous indeed. The audience always has the last word—in their mind and sometimes out loud also!

The job of the presenter is to provide an experience that technology cannot. This experience is rooted in the dynamics of person-to-person communication. No audience ever comes to a presentation saying, "I hope she tells me what I already know and makes it more complicated." Learning often happens best through an experience, not just data or PowerPoint slides. Your audience wants something from you that they can get nowhere else. Your competition for this presentation would do it differently with the exact same data. Even when hearing a scripted speech, audiences find they are more engaged by one speaker than by another.

This is the critical difference for you as presenter—you must realize the value only you can bring. This often begins through your difference—how you say things, how you word the concepts, how you envision the experience you want your audiences to have.

In corporate America today, you will rarely hear the word "problem" used in meetings. It has been replaced with the word "challenge" or "opportunity." Salespeople have known for years that when you say "no" what they really hear is "not yet"! Are these merely ways to finesse a word or does meaning, and therefore communication, really change? Does a wording change really change the meaning of what you say to a receiver?

Imagine for a moment someone introduces you to another and says, "This is Bob, he's an OK guy." Your reaction? What if the introducer says, "This is Bob, I wanted you to meet him because he is an expert in something I think you both have in common." Or how about this? "This is Bob, someone I have had the honor to work with over the past year. He makes my work look better and better and better." Are these just words or do they convey meaning?

COACH'S COMMENTS

Question: As the lead editor for the publishing company I work for, I present books to the sales force for their market positioning and feedback. How can I "say it differently" for each book I present?

Your coach says: Your key is to simplify the message of each book you present and repeat it at least twice. Borrow the most memorable phrase the author uses and tack on your own perspective. For example, this book offers practical tips with a carry-along coach (the author's words)—really unique ideas from pros who speak every week (your perspective). It's also important to add something for the audience's perspective. This book comes highly recommended for the thirty-something professional market—from the techies who rarely speak in front of an audience to the sales force who overuse PowerPoint on a daily basis.

Error! Contact not defined. Professional speaker Jim Meisenheimer (www.meisenheimer.com) recommends we never use what he calls "pathetic" words: wish for, hope for, kind of, but, if maybe, wonder if, would like to . . . all of these words are not only soft, but they convey tentativeness, even uncertainty. What if we used nonpathetic words such as yes, no, want, goal, determined, made, focused, and even the connective word "and"? When we speak, we need to do so with verbal and vocal certainty—our audiences want to know that we know and that we know we know! This happens best when you know what you are going to say and you say it.

Give the audience something to listen to, to learn from, to react to, to disagree with, even to get riled about. Often speakers are so careful of the listeners that they try to please everyone in attendance. This is a mistake. Use strategic words that convey precisely what you want to get across in the minimum amount of time. Don't go on and on and on. "Say it and sit down" has been the silent wish of many an audience member!

Here is a challenge for you. Show your value by finding new and interesting ways to say things differently than you have before and certainly differently than your audience has heard before. This makes you extremely valuable.

Have to give bad news about the budget to your boss and your boss' boss? You could say, "The numbers do not support any more initiatives" or you could say, "You pay me to solve what some people call problems. Your superiors pay you to do the same. Today we are really going to earn our money because we will be on a treasure hunt—finding the money to make our dream hospital come true." Who would you want to listen to more?

This requires that you know the receiver well enough to know the message they want and need to hear, but not so well you fail to surprise them because you are afraid of their reaction. In corporate

America today, many team members work more out of fear when presenting to their boss ("I couldn't do that!") than from creativity and innovation. This could be why so many presentations look so similar—all are rooted in fear and aim for safety. You need take no risks when you really know the receiver. Is she a sailboat captain on weekends? Does he have little children? Is your boss' boss a dog person? Knowledge is power, and knowledge allows for that innovative part of you that can create great interest for this special audience.

For any audience, no matter how smart or important—simplify, simplify, simplify. This does not mean you "dumb down" the concepts. On the contrary, it means you know this material so well that you can get to its essence. This is the heart of simplification. Steer clear of jargon. Use your own words. Speak to this audience so that they clearly hear precisely what the heart of the matter is. You will have them hounding you for autographs later!

Use your own words and say it differently.

THREE WAYS TO SAY "THANK YOU"

- **Use a thank-you by telling them what you learned from them today.** Make this your closing thought to the audience. Tell them straightforwardly what you learned from them today (rehearse in advance and use the rule of three) and simply end with a heartfelt "thank you."

- **Before you close, especially if this was a very good meeting, ask each person to say what he or she learned from it, and then thank each person for the contribution.** This works best in groups of less than eighteen in number.

- **Walk among the audience using your eyes and gestures, lightly touching a few members in the audience on the shoulder as you say your closing thoughts.** Physical proximity as long as there is no hint of sexuality is a powerful way to make the audience feel appreciated.

Part II

Prepare Like Crazy

9

Practice Is the First Priority

- **Practice sets you up for success.**
- **Practice helps you adapt and aim for usefulness, not perfection.**

The National Speakers Association of nearly four thousand professional speakers asked its members for their top tips for a successful speech. One tip received more than 35 percent of the vote for first in importance—practice! It was followed by arriving early, breathing deeply, mingling, knowing your audience and forgetting yourself. Practice, according to the pros, does more than anything else to set you up for success. Yet, when we ask our coaching clients how much they've practiced an important talk, most say, "Not enough," or worse, "Not at all." If you truly understand what practice does for you, you will not neglect to practice ever again. More important, practicing sets your audience up for success.

When you practice, don't make the mistake of focusing too heavily on memorization and perfection. Perfection is a trap. It only appears to be a worthy goal. Who wouldn't want a brain surgeon to be perfect? Or to have perfection in your own presentations, meals, parties, or life? But perfection is only a side goal and sometimes a sideshow! A successful surgery is useful. When you recover, you really don't know or care if all went "perfectly"—you only care that you are OK! Does your party have to be perfect or just fun? Does a special dinner have to be without flaw or warm and intimate? And the last presentation you sat through—were you watching for every error, or were you simply there to learn and enjoy it and use the information?

Yes, perfection is nice. However, have you ever attended a "perfect" party and not had a very good time? Have you ever visited a perfectly appointed home that wasn't so "homey"? This is why we caution you about memorizing. One slipup and you are just "not perfect"! Memorized speeches almost always sound memorized. Practiced speeches sound natural. The difference lies in the goal—is it for you or for them?

Kevin's first professional speech was supposed to be in front of twenty-five people, but twenty-five hundred showed up! He had memorized large sections of his speech, but at the last minute the night before, he made an outline of his talk in large twenty-five-point font. He had heard registration was much larger, and he thought to himself, "What if I lose my place?" Fortunately, his outline gave him the assurance he needed to follow his prepared remarks, but without the canned effect of memorization. Needless to say, he still asks himself the "what if" questions each "night before." Is he prepared? Yes. Rehearsed? Sure. Memorized? Never!

While you may not want to look like you lost your place, the real problem is that the audience took their valuable time to be with you because they believed you had used your valuable time to prepare for them. All speakers want excellent evaluations. We receive the best ones when we think "them" and not "us."

Learn a lesson from actors. An actor's rehearsal begins by sitting down around a table with the script in hand and reading it out loud with everyone else. The cast hears the characters come to life vocally, and then they talk about the writer's concepts. The following rehearsals add movement, still with script in hand. Finally, the script disappears and the actor works with props and some key costuming and set pieces. In dress rehearsal, all the makeup, props, costuming, and set pieces are present so that the actor can come as close as possible to creating the feel of opening night. On opening night, the actor is at ease, feeling comfortable in character, in costume, and in the environment. If something does go wrong during the performance, the actor is ready to improvise because he or she is so well rehearsed in the way things should be. While actors may say every single word in the script, they are "beyond memorization" because they are living the scene. They are so prepared they sound spontaneous.

As a speaker, you need to be proactive and work hard to create that same sense of comfort, usually in much less time. If you want to be able to improvise well when something goes wrong during your talk, you need to be confident with your original plan so you can momentarily put it aside. Stay familiar with your notes, your audience, and your environment. Once you have a fairly good idea of how your talk will go, practice the opening. Even practice your opening sentences the same way the actor does. Do it so many times that it becomes natural.

The first few minutes, actually the first four minutes, of your presentation are crucial, the key to the rest of the presentation. Start well and you will have your audience in the palm of your hand for the rest of the time.

Practice begins at home. As you finalize your presentation, say the words out loud. Stand up and imagine you're in front of the group. If you have visuals, use your remote. Hold the remote in your hand. Practice the speed at which you want the visuals to progress. The more important the presentation, the more you should say out loud. Many times, saying the words out loud will promote new or better ways to say things, more appropriate than your first attempt. Have a few main words that will signal the important points to you. You can even keep those words in large font type on a card in front of you. No one will see it but you and by that time you won't need it either—but it will be nice to have handy.

Practice continues in the car and everywhere. Cyndi is a master at rehearsing her opening in the car on the way to the presentation. She ignores the puzzled looks of others at the stoplight. Kevin practices his openings and his stories as he engages in natural conversation with others throughout the week—with his university students, on the airplane, with taxi drivers, and with his family. This helps him see what others think is interesting, what they think is funny, and how a particular story may elicit some emotional reaction. It helps him prepare, helps him work on sounding more spontaneous, and is a key to what particular words say and mean to others.

Practice in real time and space. The ideal scenario would allow every presenter to run through the entire presentation out loud in the room where it will be given. The pros often do this when they arrive for an event. They check in, beg a kind employee to open the room they'll be in, and scout it out—sometimes rearranging tables and chairs to promote intimacy (always up front, close together) or discussion. We find this invaluable when we present in new spaces, especially in hotels and conference centers. Truthfully, we rarely get a chance to go through the entire talk, but we can review notes, prepare charts, and practice with opening slides. This sets us up for success the next day. As with our actor colleagues, just being in the space, walking around, sitting in the farthest audience chair—all of this helps us feel more at ease. And, yes, we do all these things the night before or at least two to three hours prior to our talk—never moments before!

COACH'S COMMENTS

Question: I work with somebody who never practices and his reports always seem to be fine; he even adds little jokes and lightens the meeting. Why should he practice?

Your coach says: He doesn't know yet what an impact he could make if he did. It sounds like he's one of those lucky people who think well on their feet. So, while he is able to make a good impression, he may be able to do much more—instigate change, move to excellence, and plan a better strategy. Imagine how impressed his boss might be if he documented with thorough research or presented the results of a difficult survey. A coach's eyes can help even the best impromptu speaker be better. There may be a lot of room for growth.

You may be thinking, "But I can't ever get in the boardroom where I present at work. It's always booked." First, we would ask,

"Is it really? Is the boardroom available at six-thirty in the morning? Have you tried it then?" If you care enough, you can usually find a way to practice. Arrive early or stay late and work in the room itself with your laptop or your notes. Find the ambiance of the room. One of Kevin's clients thought this was a "little over the top" and said to Kevin, "Well, they hardly ever make personnel decisions at these meetings." Can you imagine Kevin's response?

When the gathering is personal, such as a wedding, a bar mitzvah, or a funeral, you can do the same. Ask the planner or host when the room will be open and try to arrive before the crowds. You'll look more relaxed and confident during your remarks because you'll have a feeling that you've already been there. That familiarity of place is what the actor has onstage after having rehearsed for weeks and weeks. If you need to leave your notes on the podium or at the lectern in a church, please make sure you have an extra copy of them on your person. Altar boys and girls have been known to move things at the last minute!

Practice even when you have only a few moments. Even if you arrive in the room shortly before you present, you can walk around it, test the mike, perhaps try your opening sentences with the mike, and mingle with any attendees. In most situations, chances are nobody will notice; they are all preoccupied with their own agendas. Don't be intimidated here. Meet and greet your audience as they are coming inside. Professionals do this for three reasons: it puts the audience members at ease, it relaxes them, and they give much better evaluations. Trust us on this one!

You can have a brilliant mind and stunning delivery skills, but if you don't practice, no one will notice. You'll try to wing it, and you'll only end up grounding yourself.

10

Begin So You Can Practice

- **What you say is not as important as what you say "next."**
- **What you feel is not as important as what you feel "right now."**
- **Best speakers eagerly wait to hear what they will be saying next and what their listeners are feeling right now.**
- **Preparation for this kind of a talk often happens *during* the talk and not before.**

Speakers often think the best way to prepare for a talk is to practice, practice, practice. This is only partially true. Some speakers actually write out their talk (not recommended), some give it to family and friends (really not recommended!), and some think they are at their best when they just "wing it" (really, really not recommended!). Sometimes, the best presentations come not from repeated practice, but from repeated, focused, strategic thinking about how to practice by concentrating on the audience, not on the presentation.

COACH'S COMMENTS

Question: It's really hard for me to find opportunities to speak more frequently than at the once-a-month sales presentation. How should I practice one-on-one and listen to what I say for something like this?

Your coach says: Even if it's the night before, it will help to say out loud what you plan to say the next day. Listen to your voice—its energy, its tone, and its pace. Do you sound enthused? I once worked on a type of drug with an expert whose boss told her she didn't sound enthused about the drug. She was shocked, thinking she was presenting the best research in the world on this drug. A salesperson definitely needs to be highly energized about any product or customer report. You won't hear your energy unless you speak it out loud!

For example, when you visit your doctor, do you want her focusing on each and every word she says to you, or would you prefer her to be consumed with your world, listening and thoughtfully reflecting on your experience? The same is true with speakers and presenters. An audience can smell a self-important speaker within minutes—and they will resent it. Audiences will forgive you some mistakes, but they are very unforgiving when you don't focus on them and their real-life concerns.

One professional speaker we know has a tremendous differential advantage by doing one simple thing prior to every presentation—he researches his audience. He goes to their Web site, to their professional association, to their industry and spouts statistics as he opens his talk. He has found this a surefire method for success.

We have often adapted the original plans for our presentations upon getting a feel for the climate of the room, the mood of the day, and the reaction to the speakers before us. Adaptation like this—spur of the moment—only works if a concerted first plan exists. Without a first plan, the presentation may look too improvisational and the speaker may lose credibility. Lots of practice in front of many groups gives you more and more courage to make last-minute, spontaneous changes that the audience can relate to in ways you hadn't planned.

A simple fact of presentation life is that, like heart surgeons, the more you perform the better you become—as long as you pay attention to the outcomes! Your best chance of a successful heart surgery is with a surgeon who has done *many* of them. Doctors pay attention to outcomes. The patient is supposed to improve, feel better, and not die!

Likewise, as a presenter, when you pay attention to what happens and you care about it, you will improve with each presentation. Therefore, your best, absolutely best, way to practice is to speak. Speak often, speak freely, speak here, speak there, volunteer answers, and pay attention when you are conversing with even one other person. What is happening as you interact? Watch for the feedback and you will become more and more effective.

However, too many of us fall victim to "good enough." We don't pay attention to outcomes, we focus on ourselves, and we simply don't allow enough room for improvement.

"Practice, practice, practice" is an excellent strategy as long as you do so in front of an audience.

FROM THE PROS

"The famous conductor Eugene Ormandy (longtime conductor of the Philadelphia Orchestra) once said: 'There are two types of conductors, one has his head in the score and the other has the score in his head.'

"The same can be said of speakers: The more familiar you are with the content of your talk, the more energy you can focus on being connected to your audience."

—Barry, corporate consultant

11

Tape and Time Yourself

- **The video doesn't lie.**
- **The visual of you speaking teaches immediately.**
- **A video and a coach set you surely for success.**

The camera doesn't lie. The great film actor Michael Caine wrote in his book, *Acting in Film:* "If your concentration is total and your performance is truthful, you can lean back and the camera will catch you every time; it will never let you fail." This feeling approaches what you will experience as a presenter after committing to taping and timing yourself before you speak. It is a wonderful confidence-building technique because you, like the film actor, will now have a mind memory of how you look and sound. Caine continues by personifying the camera: "She hangs on your every word, your every look; she can't take her eyes off you. She is listening to and recording everything you do, however minutely you do it." The camera doesn't lie; taping yourself is the ultimate in truth telling.

With the ease and accessibility of digital video today—both in filming and in viewing—taping is an easy and convenient process. You can bring a camera to work, set it up on a tripod, and tape yourself in a boardroom. Then look at the tape on your computer or video playback and analyze the mannerisms you want to keep and what you want to change. Depending on the capability of your system, you can save it on a DVD and send it to a coach or coworker who can help you. Our coaching clients tell us that videotaping and playback are the most valuable parts of our sessions.

> ### COACH'S COMMENTS
> **Your coach says:** Speakers tape themselves on all sizes of
> audiocassettes and digital recording devices. The Olympus DM-20
> is a favorite among the pros. Whatever your preferred mode, record
> yourself each and every time. Don't make a big production out of it.
> Just turn on the recorder and forget it is there. Later, listen to fifteen
> minutes of your talk. What did you like best and what will you do
> next time? This is all you need to do to develop the standards of a
> real pro.

The devil is in the details. What should you look and listen for
in your video? There are many things: Your vocal and body delivery, your confidence and tone, and your use of notes are some elements that coaches watch for. The video document will help you
catch any distractions—noticeable habits like hair twirling, bright
jewelry, hands in pockets, and any tendency to fill pauses with
"uhms." You'll also see how often you look down at your notes or
back at your visuals and screen in comparison to how you're able
to look out at the pretend audience.

Why should you time yourself? Timing is one of the trickiest
skills for the speaker. Like using a pause, excellent timing is the
mark of a true pro. You will speak more slowly in the real situation than you do in practice. The presence of an audience fuels extra sentences and all kinds of improvisational questions and
comments on both your end and theirs. Keep that in mind if
you're asked to provide a ten-minute summary. Practice it at
about seven minutes and you'll really have ten. This sounds odd,
but it's almost always true.

After you've watched a run-through and checked your timing,
it's a good idea to repeat your remarks again immediately. If you
don't want to run the entire talk, just practice the opening and a
few of the key persuasive points you want to make. Chances are
you'll see an improvement already that will boost your confidence.

A coach gives an expert eye. We have both coached many,
many speakers and there is not one who hasn't improved in at
least one area as a result of coaching. From ministers to VPs to

salespeople to job seekers, every presenter benefits from the perspective of an expert who listens to many speakers and gathers tips and techniques along the way. Of course, your "concentration must be total" and your "performance must be truthful." Another set of eyes and ears always yields at least one idea worth considering—even if it is your own eyes viewed through Michael Caine's lovingly personified "female" camera!

Taking the time to tape and time your presentation provides truth only a camera and clock can give.

12

Know the First Four Minutes Cold

- **If you memorize anything, consider memorizing the first four minutes.**

- **What do you most want the audience to feel during those initial moments?**

- **Use your first four minutes to find out what kind of audience you have.**

Kevin was backstage recently for a major meeting. The speaker who was about to present paced in back, speaking his opening lines over and over again, complete with gestures and facial expressions. This famous and well-respected speaker looked nervous! As the announcer began to introduce him from the stage, he stiffened, walked slowly to the edge of the stage, . . . and when they said his name, he burst onto the stage, funny and relaxed like a Bob Newhart character, roaming around with his typical "aw shucks" persona.

How could this be? He looked like a nervous wreck backstage. But onstage, he looked like he was right at home. What he understood was an age-old piece of presenter wisdom—if your first four minutes work, so will the remaining forty. Most professionals know that if they don't grab the audience within the first critical 240 seconds, there will be no second chances later on.

The book, *Contact: The First Four Minutes*, by Leonard M. Zunin, details what many of us know intuitively—first impressions are vital. Every conversation, every date, every encounter, every meeting has this built-in time—four minutes. The first four minutes are the crucial time when an audience decides if you are worth listening to. They decide on your credibility, their personal interest in you, even how engaged they will be for the rest of your presentation.

When you prepare your presentation, spend most of your time in the first four minutes, especially as you complete your final touches. In those first moments, frame your talk, tell the audience what they are about to hear and learn, and, most important, give the audience your best chance for them to like you. Knowing your first four minutes cold shows you are aware of this important speaker/audience connection time and that you plan to utilize that time wisely.

Your first impression is important. Even if your audience knows you, they still want to see who you are for the first time, this time. Never take this for granted. With typically critical audiences like physicians, engineers, or CEOs, many speakers will plan diligently to make the very best first impression and intuitively put more work into the opening. The danger comes when you know too much, assume too much, and prepare too little. This is probably true for most of life, and even more so for formal presentations.

An opposite danger is to apologize as you begin—for anything: the lighting, the sound, the late start, the long meeting, the time away from the office, or the fact they have to listen to you talk! This is such a bad habit that more than half of the speakers we coach and work with have caught it, usually from other speakers or their managers! Cyndi even coaches her teenaged son's rock band to never apologize—for the acoustics, the lack of warm-up time, or a broken string. Most of the time, the audience doesn't know or care.

Check yourself right before you begin: how you look, how you think, and what you most want. Then check one more time in the mirror. If you are with someone else, ask him or her to primp you a bit—they will! Check your thinking. Assume the best about yourself, your message, and your audience. They have come to hear only you. They want you to succeed. Picture yourself giving them a gift they can get nowhere else and from no one else. Finally, what do you want to have happen? A friend of Kevin's told him, "I assume someone in every audience is contemplating suicide and my job is to give them hope." Another said, "I remember the best teacher I ever had and I tell myself to be like him."

These final thoughts are critical for you to focus on the audience and not on yourself. Remember, audiences don't like presenters who are all about themselves. They want a presenter who listens through their words. An ironic wish for sure: Those listening want to hear from us that we are listening! This is why you will often hear someone say after a church service, "It was as if she knew just what I was thinking." This is a real compliment to a prepared presenter.

Frame your talk for optimum clarity. Some presenters say they are going to "share." Some say they want to "teach." Still others bounce onstage and no matter what they are saying, you know they are there to "get your juices flowing." Frequently in art galleries you will hear passionate debates about the frames around the artwork. Frames make or break a picture. If they draw too much attention to themselves, they distract. If they are too subdued, they become invisible. One frame can be too gaudy for some pictures and perfect for others.

Our words frame also. A simple word like "but" can set off defensiveness in the other person. "I hear what you are saying, Bob, but . . ." usually wipes out any good intention you may or may not have had toward Bob! And he won't be listening past the "but," either! What if, however, you said, "I hear what you are saying, Bob, and I would like to suggest XYZ." This is more likely to persuade Bob to unite on a common purpose, even if the two of you disagree. Do you really want to say "stupid" or are you better off using "confused, well intentioned, in need of some clarification"? Do you want to say "guys" when "gentlemen or ladies" works better?

Recently, a friend of Kevin's was prevented from entering an elevator at the Ritz-Carlton in St. Louis because Aretha Franklin and her entourage had entered. He had not noticed her; he simply knew the bodyguard was bigger than he was! As the door closed, the guard apologetically helped him to another elevator. When he inquired who was on the elevator, the guard said, "The Queen of Soul," and Kevin's friend knew who that was! What words make the biggest difference for you? Choose them well.

COACH'S COMMENTS

Question: I've memorized my first four minutes. When I practice and forget a phrase, though, I panic. How can I be totally comfortable with what I've memorized?

Your coach says: Why not give yourself permission to "goof up" a few words in your memorized opening? The world is not going to end if you say things out of order or forget a key line. When the pros do this, they find a way to get the line in later in the talk. Just keep going and nobody will notice. They have no idea what you had planned to say!

What the audience hears and learns begins with you. Tell an audience early on what your presentation is about. Be careful not to tell them too much and beware of telling them too little. Be creative. Rather than saying: "Today I want to talk to you about the best pesticide my company has to offer today's farmers," try this: "The risks are too great to continue business as usual with your old pesticides." Or perhaps, "Safer, better, cheaper—that is what today is all about." Which one grabs your attention more? Which one will grab your audience's attention more?

Remember to give them an opportunity to like you. Smile. Yes, smile. If you frown they will assume the worst—you don't like them! Even in a eulogy situation, put a slight smile on your face and mostly in your eyes. Every member of an audience, even of thousands, will see that smile in your eyes, conveyed through your words. It is not critical that all audience members like your ideas, not important that they love you, not significant that they rave about you. It is critical that you as the presenter are seen as credible, passionate, and engaged. In other words, they want to know that you know, know that you believe in what you are saying, and know that they are important to you. Therefore, give them that opening part of you that is likable as a human being. They'll be more at ease, more open to your ideas, and happier they came to listen to you.

The first four minutes are the crucial time when an audience decides if you are worth listening to. Give them the attention they deserve.

13

Give Yourself Think Time

- **Great ideas develop over time, personal time.**
- **Reflection time is precious for you *and* your audience.**

You've been asked to present. Hopefully, you've had more than a few days' notice, but even if your timeline is tight, you know you have to plan the presentation at some point. It's not going to appear out of thin air as you stand before the group. Most speakers wait too long to begin planning their talk. That is, they "wait too late" to begin thinking about their talk.

COACH'S COMMENTS

Your coach says: Before you answer a question, stop and think. Before you respond to a criticism, stop and think. Before you make an important point, stop and think. Stop by using the technique called "the pause." Think by using the question "How will they hear this?" When you stop and think, you will always give a better answer. And you will look more knowledgeable, more confident, more in charge. (Try this at home during your next family argument and see what happens!)

Take time to think. Cyndi and Kevin work differently in the writing of presentations, but not so differently in thinking about their presentations. Kevin writes closer to the performance date than Cyndi does. Cyndi starts days before, while Kevin writes and fine-tunes hours before. Both think about the presentation frequently once it's scheduled.

You may think this sounds exhausting, but it's really not. It's taking every minute of extra thought time to create. In effect, what looks like formal preparation is merely the last step of a thought process that began the day the program was agreed to. We think in the car, in the shower, just before sleep, while reading the paper—we use all of our time to prepare in an informal way. Keeping your customer, keeping your audiences on your mind continually, though informally, will only enhance your presentations.

Write your thoughts down. Once you get the assignment, jot down ideas and notes as they occur to you. These ideas may strike you at the oddest times—Cyndi once came up with the idea for an entire keynote presentation and marketing theme while jogging. She had been thinking about the nervousness corporate trainers feel the first time they facilitate a class in front of their peers and coworkers. Her thoughts led her to the silent plea that she herself had made her first time out, "If I can just make it to the first break. . . ." That idea then became the title of her presentation at many training conferences to come. Trainers told her that's exactly how they felt!

Kevin keeps a hardcover notebook of thoughts and notes as they occur to him—when he's talking on the phone, at a meeting, during a teleconference, or while eating dinner with someone. Often, he refers to the notebook for exact wording and quotes from people he has talked with. These are called "notes quotes" because many times they are the verbatim quotes from his clients. When the clients say they want an educational program, Kevin is careful never to refer to it as a motivational program. When the clients use the word "goals," these are not referred to as "objectives." Pharmacists are schooled to keep notes this way, and you can, too.

Your thoughts about a theme, a metaphor, or a slogan for a talk can occur almost anywhere, anytime. Cherish your ideas, respect them not for where they occur, but that they occurred at all! Develop them. Most audiences are delighted and surprised when what they thought would be a mundane business presentation becomes interesting and easy to remember.

Here are other ways speakers come up with ideas: on a long flight, at a traffic light, during a theatrical performance, at the doctor's office, in the dentist's chair, while walking a dog or planting bulbs, in a movie line, while reading a book, and while playing a child's game.

Don't feel you need to be a pro to use all these common, everyday situations to season your presentation. A weekly sales report can easily have a theme like "Nothing Ventured, Nothing Gained." An employee benefits presentation can benefit from a slogan like, "Your HR Department—Always on Your Side." A school fund-raiser thrives on stories of children's activities, the field trip memories and art class projects with water and clay. Consider beginning your presentation with one of these stories. However, always avoid the cliché opening line: "It's great to be in Atlanta today," or "I just flew in from California and boy are my arms tired," or the absolute killer, "I heard a great joke. . . ."

Instead, start immediately with a story. Rather than "thank you" to this and that person, take charge and begin! Tell the story! You can do your politically correct "thank yous" after the story. Grab their attention!

"We won't stomp out terrorism by merely killing today's terrorists. We must now begin to work with what causes young people to become terrorists" is a sure attention grabber. Better, how about this: "He is eight years old, he lives in Baghdad, his parents are poor, there are guns in the house, food is at a premium, his older brother was killed as an innocent bystander in a car bombing—and his mother blames the Americans. What do you think he wants to be when he grows up?" Open with a story.

Reflect on life every chance you get. There is a bit of a philosopher in all of us. A presentation should bring out the philosopher in you. To do that, you need to take time to reflect. Henry Mintzberg, author of *Managers Not MBAs: A Hard Look at the Soft Practice of Managing and Management Development*, describes a new process of

MBA achievement that allows for periods of reflection in between case studies and theory applications. Don't be apologetic about time spent daydreaming. Reflecting is vital for the creative process. In fact, this step has traditionally been called incubation—it's a valuable time where an idea takes hold and begins to grow.

You sell yourself and your client short if you don't take time to think about your presentation.

14

Find Out What Happened Last Time

- **Your success or failure with a particular audience can be guaranteed with a simple question.**

- **Asking for specifics is sometimes clumsy and embarrassing—and always worth it.**

- **History may repeat itself but as far as you are concerned, last time should never happen this time.**

Try to avoid giving presentations when you don't know what happened last time, last week, yesterday, and in the last hour. We know of too many speakers who just "show up" for their talk and give their presentation. Perhaps we should say we know of too many *mediocre* speakers who do so!

Take the time to uncover detail. The best presenters know exactly what happened because they were in attendance. They know what happened at the cocktail party the night before because they were there. They know which people are staffing what booths in the exhibit hall, who last year's speaker was, and even what the audience had for lunch moments before the start of the talk. And the best occasional presenters know where they are on the agenda, what to do if the boss goes over time, and whether or not that difficult member of the team will be present.

COACH'S COMMENTS

Question: I'm a salesperson who makes a lot of presentations on my product, software for employee benefits. I'm always reluctant to ask about "what happened last time" because I want to be a respectful competitor in my field.

Your coach says: If you don't ask, how will you know? You can always use a warm, tentative tone to ask questions such as, "Is there anything you do *not* want to hear about based on your past experiences?" or "What can I do to best build on what you already know? Do you need statistics earlier than last year's?" or "What is it you know now about your benefits-software needs that you didn't know last year?"

Why is it important to uncover this amount of detail? The answer is this—to get closer to the experience of the audience. You'd be surprised what you learn from presentations of topics that you don't understand. Kevin speaks frequently to physicians. The presenters prior to him often speak of radiology scans, pharmacy complications, and FTEs. Kevin usually has no idea about the content of these presentations. He attends them because what he does learn is so useful to his program. What does he learn? He can gauge the degree of audience interest, tiredness, and overall energy. With that knowledge, he can speak to the audience members and gain important rapport with them. Perhaps most important, the audience sees him in attendance! This becomes a huge benefit when Kevin takes the stage. Being there gives him credibility. The audience even thinks he understands what they have discussed! Maybe he does, but that's not as important as reaching closer to the audience.

Cyndi once presented an after-dinner speech to a group of customer service representatives. She did her homework and found out from the meeting planner that a member of the Chicago Bears football team had presented the year before. Usually a professional athlete presents a lighter, more motivational talk with several stories and a few content points. Cyndi understood that. What she failed to ask about was the ratio of information versus entertainment they expected and whether alcohol consumption was involved. Too late, she discovered that the hardworking reps liked their alcoholic drinks, and that entertainment was the name of the game for their speaker. In retrospect, she would have included more stories and less content in her talk. Now, she asks that question every time she is requested as an after-dinner speaker.

Even if you are presenting to your own team, engage in these same techniques. Never assume you can just stand up and speak. Ask questions, be aware of what has just happened, find out how the last meeting went from the point of view of the audience, and never assume you know better or more or differently than those you are speaking to. This way you will move into the position of learner—the best place for a teacher to be in.

Always prepare like a professional.

15

Set Yourself Up for Success

- **Nobody cares more than you.**
- **When you begin, you've begun.**
- **When you end, you're done.**

The gift of a presentation is yours. Your meeting planner will be your best ally. Nobody cares more than you about every step that will lead to your success. Cyndi's son was an award-winning Chicago-area high school soccer player. One stormy late-autumn night of his senior year, the family attended an awards ceremony for the best high school soccer players in the state. The banquet room overflowed with some four hundred players and their proud parents and grandparents. At the head table sat the state officials who introduced players and various awards.

One highlight of the evening was clearly the presentation of the Hall of Fame Award, given to a high school soccer coach who had devoted much of his life to the job. The year's award winner was introduced by his son, who after giving a loving play-by-play of his father's career, asserted, "No matter what, Dad did what a high school coach should do. Dad always kept it fun." The crowd was near tears as the coach took the podium. But instead of building on the moment, unfortunately, his first words were these: "I just flew in from Arizona and you lied about the weather here in Chicago. I thought you said it would be warm! This is awful!"

What a lost opportunity! The gift of the audience's rapt attention and the magic of the moment were in his hands. He could have said something like, "Thanks, son, you're the one who inspired me since you were a peewee player in the park district. It is truly an honor to continue to have fun with all of you gentlemen who love soccer . . ." Instead, the coach fell prey to the killer of many openings—the mundane. Don't fumble the ball by opening with the time, weather, food, or venue before you start your speech. That's terrain for C-speakers. You're better than that.

> **THREE WAYS TO ADJUST YOUR ATTITUDE:**
> - Tell yourself, "I love what I do, I know what I do, I love what I do," over and over all the way to the talk and to the podium. Few athletes go on the field thinking they will lose. Presenters cannot afford negativity as they approach the audience.
>
> - Remind yourself you are a good person doing the best you can at something most people dislike. And remember that this particular audience is investing their time to hear you—they want you to succeed.
>
> - Pat yourself on the back for showing up and smiling. Your audience deserves to have you in an encouraged place. Do that for them and for you.

You are in charge of your beginning. Nobody will help you plan your opening but you. Yes, you can research information about the audience (four hundred soccer players and their proud families who have only one chance to be present). You can understand the demographics (from all over the state and from all ethnic groups and backgrounds). You can familiarize yourself with the venue (a large suburban banquet hall with a head table, podium, and a mike). But it's up to you to imagine this and put it all together in your opening. Set yourself up for success. Be prepared with the first words out of your mouth. Say them in the car on the way there, mouth them in the restroom, but whatever you say, don't start with, "Thank you for coming tonight." How boring is that? Here are some alternatives:

- **Make a definitive statement.** "I practiced soccer 3,452 afternoons in my life. And they were all worthwhile."

- **Ask a question.** "What do we all have in common? Boys who like soccer balls—kicking them, heading them, dribbling them."

- **Stir the emotions.** "Clearly, I'm not the only dad here tonight who loves soccer and loves his son."

Don't throw away your last words. The C-speaker says, "Thanks again for coming. Have a great evening. Enjoy dessert." The pro knows the value of the last moments and wouldn't dream of mentioning dessert. Besides, most audiences want to come or have to come and don't need to be thanked for coming.

At the soccer awards banquet, the Hall of Fame–winning coach did a much better job with the ending. After receiving the award and reviewing the highlights of his career wins, he mentioned several players who became pros or semipros along the way. Each honor or win or famous player made a stronger and stronger point. Each, he said, was a memorable event or person. "I've had a wonderful career, but this induction into the Hall of Fame is priceless." His last words honored the event, the audience, and the award.

Never throw away your last words. When *Titanic* won the Oscar for Best Picture, the director accepted with an emotion-laden account of the decision to do the film, the lives lost in the actual event, and the hours of labor on the part of the actors and crew. Then, right when he had the audience in the palm of his hand, he raised the trophy and yelled, "Now let's party 'til dawn!" What a mistake. He destroyed the moment and lessened the impact of history with one silly sentence. When you end, you're done!

**Success in speaking is up to you and only you—
from the very beginning to the very end.**

FROM THE PROS

"No matter how tight a schedule you are on, always plan to arrive at least an hour prior to your talk. If you get stuck in traffic or get lost, you'll still be on time, and most of the time, you'll arrive early. That gives you a chance to check out the room and PA system, change the arrangement of chairs and set up the front/stage/riser/podium the way you like it, and get yourself a glass of water, if you want one. Once everything is set up, you can greet and chat with audience members."

—Rita, professional speaker, author, procrastination expert

COACH'S COMMENTS

Your coach says: So you're wondering if you can ever overcome your jitters. As you prepare for your presentation, you may want to consider and rehearse your opening line. In it, have the seeds of your opening thought as well. For example: "Thank you for your attendance today at such an extraordinary event. I say extraordinary because what we will be engaged in over the next three days will truly be different and not at all ordinary. We are here to XYZ." In this way, your opening sentences are linked to your main idea, providing you a way to enter your speech smoothly. The chance of too much pausing or being flustered is greatly reduced. All speakers have jitters; they just know how to deal with them.

The old adage is that everyone has "butterflies in their stomach when they speak; pros just know how to make them fly in formation!" Pick a few words as your opening words and say them first. Don't try to be spontaneous, extemporaneous, or cute, but simply begin with the words you have rehearsed. They might be "Today I . . ." or "Did you ever . . . ?" These opening trigger words will help you get through the first sentence and the first five minutes and the next ten and finally to the end. The trigger words ensure success because they are the beginning of what you already know. Save being spontaneous for after the speech when the audience is telling you how great you are. Instead, "seem spontaneous" by being so well rehearsed that your speech just flows.

Part III

Respect the Client

16

Know Who the Real Client Is

- **Your real client is always the person who asked you to give the presentation.**
- **It makes no difference if the audience loved your talk—your real client has to love it, too.**
- **Real clients rarely know what they need; they know only what they want.**

Of course you want to communicate with the audience; however, they are not your primary clients. You need to be clear with your audience, and it is critical to satisfy your audience; however, they are not the final evaluators of your success. Your real client is the person who asked you to give this presentation. Period.

COACH'S COMMENTS

Question: If I'm presenting to the upper management of my company, who is my real client?

Your coach says: The real client is the person who is responsible for you being there and not someone else. If it's the president, then that's your client. If it's his secretary, then he's your client. Your client is the person who has the ability to make the decision to invite you to speak again and whose career or at least reputation for good judgment is on the line if you are less than stellar.

Kevin hired a professional speaker (whom he had heard many times before) to speak to the faculty where he belonged. The man was a dynamic and effective speaker. Still, as they rode from the airport to the school together, the car became quiet. The speaker said, "Kevin, are you afraid I'm going to screw up?" Both laughed. Kevin answered, "I just want them to like you and learn as much from you as I have." The speaker said, "They will and they'll thank you for it." He was right.

Again, it is essential to remember the real client is the person who has put him- or herself on the line for you. If you are a team member, your client may be your team leader; if you are a librarian, your client may be the community leader who funded the library; if you are the father of the groom, your client is most likely the newlywed couple.

These people act as your pipeline to the audience. One presenter we know brings his real client into the room as the audience is filing in and quietly asks, "Tell me about these people individually." The client then shares things like, "The fellow in the red shirt is a terrific salesperson, a real star. The woman in blue is a bit put out that she has to take time off for this today. The CEO is in the blue suit and if he stays for the entire lecture, you will win my loyalty forever!"

These are priceless comments. They are also spontaneous and extremely helpful to the speaker. The presenter may never refer to them, but at least knows who is who. Having regular eye contact with the CEO is likely to keep him in the lecture hall!

Your real client hired you and it is the real client, not the audience, who will rehire you . . . or not!

17

Know What the Meeting Planner *Really* Wants

- **Ask questions until you're perfectly clear.**
- **What they say and what they want may be two different things.**
- **Always check back one last time.**

Your meeting planner may not be the traditional full-time kind that the pros work with; your planner may be your boss, your associate, or your father-in-law to be. Whoever they are, it's your job to find out what they want. One of the National Speakers Association's Meeting Planners of the Year gave this advice to speakers as part of her acceptance speech: "Always do more than you get paid for." This begins by asking lots of thorough questions. Questions are the key to knowing what the meeting planner wants.

Don't assume anything. Meeting planners all have three things in common: 1. They are busy. 2. They expect you to know what to do. 3. They have other priorities. Think of your future father-in-law. Do you suppose your toast is first on his to-do list? Think of your boss. Is your sales presentation weighing heavily on her mind? Does your project team leader prioritize your talk near the top of his responsibilities? Actually, the pro has a certain advantage here because an experienced full-time meeting planner knows how to ask and answer important questions about the goals of the presentation and the needs of the audience. But you still need to ask. Never assume your meeting planner has thought through every last detail.

COACH'S COMMENTS

Question: What if I expected positive outcomes and the meeting planner doesn't have any?

Your coach says: Then it's your job to dig deeper. Perhaps the word *outcome* is unfamiliar or too strong for your planner. Simply probe by asking, "What do you hope will happen after the meeting when they go back to work?" or "How can my presentation help them achieve their sales goals?" or "What problem is it that I'm helping to solve?"

Cover both the shallow and the deep end. The obvious or "shallow end" questions are:

- **How long do I have to speak?**

- **If we're running overtime in the program, how do you want me to adjust—finish no matter what or cut the speech to fit the time?**

- **Tell me about the audience.**

- **Who speaks immediately before me?**

- **What happens when I am finished?**

- **Will there be food or drink? How much and when? Has alcohol been a factor with this group previously?**

- **How much humor would you like?**

- **What percentage of this is entertainment? What percentage is information? How about inspiration?**

Then, go to the "deep end" or big-picture questions like these:

- **What do you want them to do as a result of this program?**

- **If I'm successful, what three outcomes will we see?**

- **Who is the main person I need to persuade, affect, or please?**

- **What do you want them to be as a result of this program?**

- **Has this topic met with successful outcomes in the past? Why or why not?**

- **What is the audience's greatest fear? Greatest happiness?**

- **What will make this talk particularly memorable?**

No matter who you're working with, if you take the time to find out the answers, your chances of success are much higher. If the planner doesn't know, find out the person to call or e-mail who can help you. In the event of a wedding, call someone else who knows your father-in-law well and can share a surprise story. If you're representing your project team, do a quick survey of the team via e-mail on an important point. Administrative assistants are always valuable sources of general information about people they work for and with. They do not want to be embarrassed, however—they still have to live with the boss when you are gone! Ask the meeting planner to give you the names of three people to call.

Many pros have these FAQs—frequently asked questions—on their Web sites. Check out Cyndi's Web site (www.cyndimaxey .com) for the ones she uses on a regular basis. Kevin always asks what the audience's greatest challenge is. You can imagine how this one question can lead to a multilayered response. Create your own list of FAQs for your presentations.

It's also important to check back as the presentation gets closer. Did anything change? Is the purpose still the same? Is it the same audience and theme, at the same time and place? Don't become a victim of poor communication about change. You're the one in front.

Some speakers even ask questions right up to the moment they present. One of Kevin's favorite speakers stands in front of the presentation room with the meeting planner and asks about each person entering the room—and anecdotes spill out of the planner's mouth!

Successful speakers ask the right questions in the right way, right away.

FROM THE RANKS

"I plan a lot of meetings for our building code officials association. I never realized the importance of speakers who really do their homework until I asked a member of the police force to present to ninety of our members on verbal judo. Right before he went on, the officer turned to me and asked, 'Now, just what does a building code official do?' "

—Don, program chair, suburban building code officials conference

---

18

Know What the Audience Needs

- **Wants and needs are not the same.**
- **The audience knows how to tell you.**
- **Your job is, of course, to listen!**

Sometimes a sales audience wants a "motivational" speech, but what they need are the skills to continually motivate themselves. Other times a more academic audience wants content, skills, and a no-nonsense approach to a topic, but what they need is a learning environment with some fun in it. And, of course, there is always the Rotary or Jaycee audience who asks you to say a few words because they think they want a speaker for their lunch when what they really need is an opportunity to talk with one another.

Wants and needs are not always the same thing. Often, in fact, they are quite different. That is why it is critical that you as the speaker know the difference and make sure you give them both—what they want and what they need. You'll get paid or thanked for giving them what they want. You'll be applauded and remembered for giving them what they need.

COACH'S COMMENTS

Question: I'm confused by what the audience wants and needs. Can you help me with my team? I'm a team leader for an electronics company. We're charged with a new product launch.

Your coach says: Your team may say they want you to present the latest competitive data. What they may really need is a chance to vent about the project and its status. They may be feeling overworked and underappreciated. While the latest competitive data will certainly help them, it won't address their need to feel appreciated. So, address the needs early on by complimenting them and praising each individual in some small way.

Kevin gave a eulogy once for a young mother who died without warning. The line to greet her husband at her wake was more than two hours long—four thousand people signed the condolences book. When asked to speak, Kevin was told what the audience wanted, "We want you to give the eulogy because you knew her." But what the audience needed was a time to laugh, cry, and pray together. So, Kevin gathered his own thoughts and then spent some time at the wake asking two questions of the many there: "What do you remember about her, and what would you say about her if you were speaking tomorrow at the funeral?"

Armed with those quotes, he essentially read them back to the audience as a part of his eulogy the next day. What they wanted were Kevin's thoughts. What he felt they needed were their own thoughts. Wisely, he gave them both.

One of Cyndi's management seminars for a large truck parts distributorship was about to begin when her meeting contact, the regional manager, approached her. "We've just had some news that I need to share with the guys before you begin. Our CEO has just announced his resignation." Cyndi was surprised, but the manager said this CEO had indicated before that he'd be around only a few years, then move on. While the regional manager was talking to the group, Cyndi had a few minutes to think, "What will these managers need now? How will this change my approach as a presenter? What should I say to make today relevant to their needs?" She decided to focus on change, and that while this change was a big one, it was only one of many that all managers faced every day.

This may happen to you as well. Your contact may change things so that you have to brainstorm what the audience needs at that moment in time. They may need to be brought together in some way, become acquainted, share common fears, ask questions, deviate from the planned agenda, or perhaps totally change course.

You can do this with any presentation at any time if you will only consider carefully wants and needs. You can do this with your meeting planner. Simply ask the question: "What do you think this group wants to hear from me? What do you think they most need to hear?" As the speaker, it is always your responsibility to address the right questions to the right people ahead of time—even moments before your presentation. You will be in a better, closer position to your audience whenever you do. This simple way of reducing your presentation to the essentials will yield the thanks of the audience as well as their applause.

It is always the speaker's responsibility to uncover audience needs prior to the speech.

THREE THINGS TO LEARN FROM ENTERTAINERS:

- They know the value of the smile—so should you.

- They ramp up their energy level right before they go on.

- They know this audience is all they have in this time and in this place.

19

Know What to Use and What to Lose

- **Shorter is (almost) always better than longer.**
- **There is a magic that surrounds the rule of three.**
- **Go back to your purpose frequently.**

Have you ever heard an audience member say, "Gee, I wish that speaker had gone on longer?" Chances are, you have rarely heard that comment. Most listeners are busy and typically less involved in your presentation than you are, no matter how committed they are to being there. Tell the stories you need to tell in as short a time as possible. After twenty minutes, most listeners have left you. The higher level the executives, the less time you should take in front of them—but use that time wisely! Executives tell us all the time that the best presenters keep the message in a form the executives can easily pass on at their level for decision making. Being brief does not in any way mean you lose any of your message or that you eliminate your stories.

Look at your lists. You know from your own experience that lists are easy to make but difficult to listen to. Remember the last time you watched list after list go by on slide after slide? An easy way to edit any talk, whether it is three minutes or three hours, is to look at your lists of things. First, look at how many lists you have. If you have a talk filled with lists, you're going to be boring. Edit those lists and vary them with analogies or stories or examples that say the same thing. Next, look at how many items are on your lists. If you have more than five to seven items, you're going to lose your listeners.

For example, if you're listing sales objectives or customer responses, look at the items you're listing and ask yourself if they can be combined or eliminated. They almost always can; you can put the full list in a handout to pass out after the talk if you feel people need the whole thing. When primitive men drew on caves about the hunt, they didn't draw every buffalo in the herd, just a group to represent all the buffalo. All the listener needs to see is the group—a representation of the buffalo.

A list of ten can sometimes work if it's cleverly designed, like David Letterman's famous "Top Ten" lists with which he began his show for a number of years. It can work if it's a list of memorable words or sentences that grab the audience's attention. But remember, if we said, "There are ten reasons you should buy this book," wouldn't they have to be pretty spectacular or clever to keep your attention? Well, here they are: 1. Your success. 2. Your success. 3. Your success. 4. Your success . . . you get the idea.

Being selective is a key component here. Kevin once heard that a fifty-seven-year-old speaker wanted to communicate his wisdom to a group and started by saying: "There are fifty-seven things I've learned in this life. Number one . . ." Most of the audience left by number twelve!

COACH'S COMMENTS

Question: I'm not very good at editing my own writing. Once I work hard on a presentation, it all looks good to me! Any advice?

Your coach says: Kathleen Passanisi, a successful professional speaker, tells a very funny story about a day in college gone wrong. This hilarious account of true multiple mishaps is always one of the highlights of her keynote speech. She shared with us how editing made it funnier; she trusted the feedback she received from colleagues that the story was too long. So now she leaves out the post-sleet storm/wet, dripping madras scarf portion. While very funny, it was anticlimactic. She understands that now. Always try to ask for feedback from trusted colleagues, a good coach, your clients, and your audiences.

Instead, concentrate on the rule of three. We are strong advocates for the rule of three. Three is an important number that unifies, clarifies, and strengthens. For example, in ancient Irish mythology, Celtic heroes traveled in three to do good throughout the land. For every talk you give, find a way to mention three ideas or thoughts or reasons somewhere in the talk. Here are some examples:

- **In a eulogy: Three reasons I'm glad I knew Joe Brown.**

- **In a toast: Three keys to love and happiness I learned from Mom.**

- **In a briefing: Three reasons to listen today.**

- **In an after-dinner humorous speech: Three reasons not to have children. (Smile.)**

- **In a technical presentation: Three reasons I'm excited about this drug.**

- **In a sales presentation: Three ways we have turned the technology around.**

- **In a training presentation: Three things you can do immediately when you go back to your telephones.**

Your purpose will keep you clear. When Cyndi's friend Cheryl turned sixty, she invited fifty-nine people to her birthday party. As the guests arrived, they were each given a list of fifty-nine characteristics—each different—that described one of the people in the room. The trick was to meet and mingle so you would learn something about everyone. The list ranged from things like "Cheryl's favorite godchild" to "climbed Machu Picchu." People had fun, and one or two actually completed all fifty-nine, but the best part was the way Cheryl handled the answers. As she pointed out each person and their featured characteristic, she added a loving, personal comment. The result was that a list of fifty-nine, which could have been tedious, became a wonderful affirmation of friendship and long relationships. Cheryl brilliantly fulfilled her purpose—to take the spotlight off herself and shine it on the guests and friends who had enriched her life.

There may be a time when it makes sense to read a list of fifty-nine—and you too may decide to do it. As long as your purpose is crystal clear, you can remain on track. This book has more than fifty-nine chapters. That could be overkill. But if we're doing this right—if we're true to our purpose—you will hardly notice because each chapter will grab your interest fully. Then you'll select when and how to proceed with the others.

Children can watch a favorite video over and over. Winning salespeople can listen to praise over and over. If you're clear about your final outcomes—what you want the audience to do and be when you are done speaking—then you will know what to focus on and what to take out of your presentations.

The more you connect, the longer you can talk.

20

Be an Expert on the Culture

- **Every company is different, in its own unique way.**

- **To employees, culture is as important as the quality of water is to fish.**

- **When presenters understand the culture from the inside out, they can help transform it.**

If you can ever take an opportunity to visit the company or division you are presenting to prior to the event, do it! How? Arrive the day or night before. Can you visit the main office? Is the cafeteria still open? If it's a conference or trade show, can you walk around the exhibit hall? Do so. Eat the food. Visit the bathrooms, walk the hallways, look in the cubicles, and speak with the administrative coordinators, janitors, and waiters. Why go to all this trouble? Because the internal culture of an organization is so obvious and yet so subtle that without this knowledge, you can easily step into a minefield. Culture powerfully impacts the life of every employee in your audience.

COACH'S COMMENTS

Question: I'm a twenty-one-year employee of a large financial services company. I probably know this company's culture better than anyone. How can I convince my newer managers that I can help them get attention because I know the ropes?

Your coach says: The best way to convince them is to allow them to see your perspective for themselves. If you begin with words like, "In my twenty-one years here, I've never seen blah blah blah," you may put them on the defensive. But if you ask a question like, "Have you considered that we're an aging group—averaging in our early fifties? That wasn't always the case. How do you think that will affect the employee buy-in of this program?"

Listen to titles and jargon. Is this audience made up of "sales-people" or "sales professionals" or "associates" or "coordinators" or any of a hundred specialty titles? You, their presenter, better know. Do they use "secretaries" or "administrative assistants" or "administrative coordinators" or simply "a/cs"? Do they revere the product they sell? (Many companies almost worship their products.) If so, listen carefully to how they speak about their product—their hamburgers, their airplanes, or their ball bearings. Never minimize what they do, how they make their product, who they are, or why they do it. It is, of course, their lifeblood!

Be clear about the titles, pronunciations, jargon, and names of executives. When you hear these references, jot them down on the inside of the file folder that holds your notes so you can, just before you begin, take one last glance at the important words and people. Cyndi once arrived early for a presentation and saw poster signs with an event sponsor's name. Because she saw this in time, she was able to meet the sponsor and to mention his organization's benefits during her talk. Perhaps even more important, she had time to become aware of the culture of sponsorship that her immediate client had long supported.

Because you have visited prior to your talk or arrived early enough to do some scouting around, you will have felt the culture and been a part of it. That will help more than anything—you'll know because you will have experienced it.

For his grocery chain client, Kevin made sure he visited five stores in very different neighborhoods, spoke to the managers, got the "tour" and experienced firsthand what the employees experienced. His best laugh line came from a comment about their break room—off-limits to the regular customers.

Departments in your own company have cultures, too! Even if it is your own company in the audience, your boss, your boss's boss, and their science or marketing people, make sure you call some people ahead of time, visit if you can, have them show you their spreadsheets, their labs, their newest designs. Ask about their challenges, difficulties, opportunities, as well as about the holiday party, the summer employee picnic, the latest construction on the new building, and where they went to school. If you speak to physicians, ask how they selected their specialty (often based on a favorite mentor), their school adventures, and their practice. Attorneys love to discuss cases, to the extent they can legally. Teachers light up when they discuss strategies that worked in their classrooms. Managers enjoy discussing challenges with their teams.

Speakers who use their knowledge and experience of an organization's culture wind up using the right words at the right time to not only gain credibility, but also to enhance the experience of the audience.

FROM THE RANKS

"Remember Bill Clinton's 'It's the economy, stupid'? Well, 'It's about the audience.' It's not about me. It's *all* about the audience. Talk less, interact more. Get your ego out of the way."

—Brian, college fund-raising professional

21

Know What Works with This Client

- **Find out with your eyes. Watch this client.**
- **Find out with your ears. Listen to this client.**
- **Discover what doesn't work. Ask this client.**

As professional speakers, one of our biggest lessons in designing effective presentations is to become unfailing, nonstop observers of everything that surrounds the culture of our clients. We learn primarily from watching and listening. Much of what we learn about is what doesn't work. (Clients will usually tell you what does work before they tell you what doesn't work. Occasionally, the opposite is true, too!) The best presenters always ask, "What is one thing I definitely should not do or say in this presentation?" or "What would make you cringe?" They ask about past problems and lessons learned, and they encourage the client to remember and to be candid. This is critical. Ask questions designed to help clients dig into their experience and their fears so you will know what is really going on for them.

    Find out on a scale of one to ten what they expect. Brian Palmer, owner of a large speakers' bureau outside of Chicago, once told us this about meeting planner clients: "They want you to be a professional speaker, but they don't want you to be a professional speaker." This is a perfect example of the difficulty of learning what works. Your client may not be able to explain it. What Brian meant is that some aspects of the pro are in demand: knowledge, excellent delivery, customization skills, dynamism, and connection. But others are never wanted: ego, over-rehearsed delivery, overused content, detail overkill, ego . . . did we say ego twice? Yes! Similarly, it's up to you to figure out if they really want you to be a technical expert. How technical? How expert? Or, if you are a salesperson—how salesperson-like do they expect you to be?

Ask them to give you a number from one to ten so you have a sense of what works in their culture. How strong should you be? What language should you use or avoid? Kevin often asks his clients to give him ongoing feedback during coffee breaks and at lunch. Better to find out while you can still do something about it, than after the event!

When meeting planners watch videotapes of potential speakers, they watch the speakers they're seriously considering much longer than others. They will watch twenty minutes of video compared to only a few minutes of someone they don't relate to. This not only reinforces the importance of first impressions, but it also solidifies how quickly clients can tell us what they like! They're searching for something and they know what it is; we have to find a way to help them communicate to us what they want.

Watch and listen. When we enter a new client environment, we begin observing immediately. How friendly is it? Who's in charge? Who has position power? What kinds of things are said? How open are people about their work and especially their mistakes? Cyndi once observed the company president referring to the warehouse employees by the colors of their shirts—blue shirts and black shirts. When she asked about this, the employees said they were accustomed to these labels and not bothered, but Cyndi would never have recommended referring to employees in this manner. Every client has a culture to observe and respond to.

We have observed telemarketing rooms where customers were lambasted once the phone was hung up or sophisticated teams where the boss was criticized by everyone—but not directly. The presenter's job is a tough one—sleuth, spirit, and gatherer.

COACH'S COMMENTS

Your coach says: There is only one way to investigate your audience's needs. Ask. You can attend lunches prior to your talk with only this question in mind: "What does this group need to hear? What works with them? Who did they have last time and how did it go?" All of this, of course, is very conversational, and very purposive. Beware not to let this information take you offtrack. Use follow-up questions such as, "What is the most challenging part of your work?"

Ask those who went before. Many presenters forget that someone almost always preceded them in a similar fashion. Ask about last year's keynoter. Inquire about the previous month's sales presentation. Take advantage of the experienced person's expertise and use it. He or she probably learned something from presenting to the group that can be shared to help you. Kevin once followed a legendary speaker a year later—every reader of this book would recognize the name. When Kevin asked the planner how it went, the planner went into great detail to make sure that Kevin did *not* in any way resemble the previous speaker. For many reasons, things had not worked out. A year later, the planner still had plenty to say about it. Never assume!

The more you know, the better impact you'll be able to make.

Part IV

Break the Rules

22

You Don't Have to Be Perfect

- **Being you is more important than being perfect.**
- **If you go "off-course," get right back on.**
- **Set up a relationship with the audience that allows for imperfection.**

Professional speakers strive for excellence. They practice the words, the timing, and the delivery of their talks. They research the audience; they energize the audience; they mix and mingle. And, in spite of all of this, they know things will probably not go perfectly. They understand it is more important to make a lasting impact than to give a perfect presentation. Every speaker we know, without exception and including ourselves, has had something go wrong. Yet we can tell you that some of the best moments we have in front of groups have been moments when we have survived mistakes, unexpected reactions, or untimely events. We like the words of business consultant and coach Nido Qubein: "Life is about impact." Yes! Make an impact with your presentations!

When you think about impact rather than perfection, your whole mood and emphasis changes. Impact makes a difference for someone else; perfection makes it all about you. Successful speakers understand that through their own imperfection is a path to trust, help, and collaboration with others. Strive for impact in your speaking and presenting and show the audience you are focused on them.

Be yourself. If you are in front of a group or waiting to go next and something goes wrong, everyone watches you. Don't think for a minute they're not. They are! Swallow your pride, breathe through your anger, gather your senses, and move on. Don't over-apologize. Don't say you're embarrassed. Don't waste time. Just move on. Watch comedians and celebrity interviews on television. When they make a mistake, they move on. They don't wait and wonder and hope; they just move on.

Ramp up rapport building now—with your "bounce-back" ability. Memorable speakers are effective because they build a natural rapport, no matter what. They apologize quickly, if necessary. They find out later what went wrong and how to make it better. This short anonymous anecdote illustrates the kind of bizarre yet funny things that happen and how important it is to laugh at them.

A CEO was scheduled to speak at an important convention so he asked one of his employees, Jenkins, to write him a punchy twenty-minute speech. When the CEO returned from the big event, he was furious. "What's the idea of writing me an hour-long speech?" he demanded. "Half the audience walked out before I finished." Jenkins was baffled. "I wrote you a twenty-minute speech," he replied. "I also gave you the two extra copies you asked for."

The lesson? Always review your notes or your PowerPoint presentation—you are the final determiner of what will guide you! If you wonder if you have repeated yourself, ask the audience! They will know. If you wonder if you are going fast enough or slow enough, ask. They know. And if you want to know what they know, ask a good open-ended question and *then listen.*

Things will go off-course. Jerilyn Willin is a consultant and speaker who also owns Old English sheep dogs trained as show dogs. Once at a major dog show, her oldest dog, Greta, unexpectedly jumped over the barricades and ran aimlessly around the show arenas. Over the loudspeaker came: "Dog off-course! Dog off-course!" As the day progressed, Greta's behavior did not improve, and the announcement "Dog off-course!" was made repeatedly. By the end of the show, the judges knew the dog so well that the announcement became: "Greta off-course. Greta off-course." Jerilyn is able to laugh now, but as a result of this "off-course" behavior, Greta is currently on hiatus from the show arena!

As a speaker, you may also go "off-course." The reaction to your ideas may be more negative than you expected; the crowd may be in a less mellow mood than you're accustomed to; your stories may fall flat, or you may have questions that begin as soon as you do. Your boss may change the strategy at the last minute; your new coworker who is copresenting with you may try to take the spotlight. You will have to adapt in the moment and in a professional manner. Then later, like Greta, you can take a break and regroup. Aim for flexibility in these kinds of situations. Speakers and presenters who insist on having things "their way" usually lose in the long run—they lose their audience.

Adapt on the spot. Ask questions and be honest. If you don't understand why you're off-course, say so. Ask what you could do differently. Then do something. Poke fun at yourself: "If I only had a brain . . ." or "If only I weren't numerically challenged!" Thank the audience for pointing out a crucial detail. Jump to the ending. Summarize three key ideas and take a short break. Ask everyone to share one word that describes his or her reaction to what happened.

Once we listened to a speaker at a major conference on Valentine's Day. Suddenly fire alarms started going off! The hotel's announcement to stay in place was made, and the speaker, who had now been interrupted three times by the alarms, regrouped by saying, "Those were probably from my mother; she has this way of reminding me to send her flowers today. . . ." It was a great way of adapting to what could have been a disorienting moment.

COACH'S COMMENTS

Question: I have to present to a new highly technical audience, and I've been told they're very analytical and unforgiving. What if something not so perfect happens? Won't they be critical?

Your coach says: Most truly technical audiences know they are technical audiences. While they do expect excellent research and documentation, they don't expect to agree with everything you say. They also don't expect you to know the answers to all their very intelligent questions. In fact, they often like to stump the presenter because it makes them look smarter! So, when you make mistakes with these crowds, apologize quickly and move on.

We know a pro who has a health-care background, yet is hired again and again by a large aircraft carrier corporation. The analytical engineers and pilots enjoy the stress-free style of this speaker. So, your technical group may be more forgiving than you think.

Set up a give-or-take relationship. Recently a management consultant introduced himself and his talk, and then added how he expected interaction from us. "You cannot hurt my feelings by disagreeing with me," he said. "I've been married thirty-eight years." That moment of humor allowed us insight into him as well as clarity of our role as audience members during his presentation. We were allowed to disagree!

When someone disagrees with you, make sure the first words out of your mouth are "thank you." Audience members like to be appreciated and they like to feel safe. When they stick out their neck, make sure they find an appreciative you at the other end.

Put it in perspective. As William Shakespeare wrote in *As You Like It*, "All the world's a stage, and all the men and women merely players." As a speaker, you have an entrance and an exit. You're not onstage forever. This is one presentation among a lifetime of events. Keep your sense of humor. Learn from the mistake, but move on. Cyndi keeps a sign on her file cabinet that reads, "The person who never makes a mistake probably isn't doing anything."

Learning is the issue here. As you rack up experience with presentation after presentation, you will increase your learning. Treat each presentation or speech as a learning experience and not as a final judgment. Mistakes are for learning.

<blockquote>The speaker who never makes a mistake
probably isn't speaking much.</blockquote>

THREE WAYS TO KEEP A DISCUSSION GOING
- **Say "tell me more"** with an interested, expectant look on your face and then . . . *wait* for them to answer!

- **Call people by name and ask them to share their perspective.** Do this only if they give you a nonverbal sign they are with you or want to participate. Never call on someone cold—they usually have no idea what you are talking about and it can embarrass them. Better yet, allow everyone to talk to a partner first, and then ask for input—you will always get it.

- **Save a few questions to ask when you really need them.** Have them prepared in advance, written on your friend the flipchart, and ask. If no participants respond, have a rehearsed story or a "before I get your response, I don't want to forget to tell you about" story ready about the last time you asked this question. Make it either serious or humorous.

FROM THE PROS

"As I do a lot of seminars where I provide facts and guidance, I learned early on not to expect to be perfect. I offer a 'guarantee' with all my presentations. In the unlikely event I don't know the answer, I thank them for the interesting question and tell them that I want to know the answer too. I get their e-mail, research the question during my (increasingly scarce) downtime, and provide them with the answer."

—John, government training and development expert

23

It's OK to Surprise Your Audience

- **Memorable presenters do things differently.**
- **Excellent research precedes reasonable risk taking.**
- **Creativity is rarely as risky as you may think.**

A winner of the National Toastmaster of the Year Award began his winning speech by falling face forward onto the floor. Afterward, he said he was afraid he'd fall flat on his face during his speech . . . and darned if he did! His point was how we're all afraid of the next step—of falling flat on our faces, but when we take that step, it feels so good. Because of his physical ability, he was able to surprise his audience with this unexpected fall. You may not be able to literally fall facedown, but you can certainly surprise your audience. As the Toastmaster winner added: "To do risky things in life, sometimes you have to take out your brain and jump on it!" Brains can get pretty logical. Don't forget to inject fun into them. Actually, consider it risky to be too safe!

Surprises come in many ways. Find the fun or unusual facts and statistics surrounding either your profession or that of someone in your audience. Architects understand proportion instinctively and search for a rule of proportion called the Golden Mean. The Golden Mean describes a relationship between two lengths, 1 to 1.1618. The Parthenon, for example, was 1.1618 times as wide as it was tall. The Golden Mean is amazing in that it appears repeatedly in nature: The second finger bone is 1.1618 times the length of the first, and so on. Think of all the fun you can have knowing this! You can say you've been searching for the Golden

Mean but only found the brass one. You can give prizes for three spontaneous examples of the Golden Mean.

Create your own or research a list of top ten questions about something. For example, you could cite the top ten questions asked by visitors to the Louvre—an easy statistic to find. Most people think the top question is "Where is the Mona Lisa?" but it's actually "Where is the women's restroom?" That may lead to a lively discussion about assumptions, tourists, customer service, or travel.

Use a prop to illustrate a concept. Cyndi once presented a proposal to a group of decision makers with a can of paint and a paintbrush. She used the story of her trial-and-error experience with her father's oil-based paint as a young girl, learning to clean the brush carefully and repeatedly. Cyndi's message to the group that day was how things worth learning well take time, tools, and coaching. To this day, she remembers exactly how to stir a can of paint and how to clean a brush well. Speaker and successful business consultant Nido Qubein uses a small bird balanced on a pointed object to illustrate the importance of balance in life. Sometimes the bird is visible as he begins; other times he reveals it from behind the podium.

Find a jolt—something that delivers a powerful wake-up call. Force your listeners to reexamine their assumptions. Jolt material can be found anywhere. With one click from the Bureau of Labor Statistics home page (www.bls.gov), we found these statistics as we wrote this book: The youth population, aged sixteen to twenty-four, will grow 7 percent over the 2002–2012 period. As the Baby Boomers continue to age, the group aged fifty-five to sixty-four will increase by 43.6 percent or 11.5 million persons, more than any other group. Number of those aged thirty-five to forty-four will decrease, reflecting the low birth rates following the Baby Boom generation.

Imagine the ways you could jolt your monthly sales meeting with statistics that are current and not hard to find. Your trade or profession most likely has several affiliated associations that have Web sites to access for detailed information. The training and development folks can go to the American Society for Training & Development site, www.astd.org. Construction specifications people can rely on the Construction Specifications Institute site, www.csinet.org. Dentists go to the American Dental Association site, at www.ada.org, and meeting professionals to the Meeting Professionals International Web site, at www.mpiweb.org. The list goes on and on. Search sites like Google and Yahoo can help you find the site you want.

COACH'S COMMENTS

Your coach says: How far should you go? Just remember here not to blindside your planner or your boss. Use your good judgment and take a considered risk, not a wild one. Err on the side of the audience's understanding, not on the side of your grandstanding.

Use interactive storytelling or song lyrics to unite an audience. Professional speakers often get very large groups involved by using these techniques. Most audiences will recognize a nursery rhyme: "Mary had a little lamb, its fleece was white as snow, and everywhere that Mary went"—let the audience finish. You can then use it to illustrate your point—followership, leadership, politics, loyalty, outplacement help, etc. Lyrics to the Beatles songs, holiday songs, and children's games are usually universal. If you're speaking to a particular age group, use the lyrics of the idols of their youth, whether it is Johnny Mathis, Jimmy Hendrix, Madonna, or Jessica Simpson.

Show a short video clip or a montage of photos. Use a clip from a movie or documentary, or make your own. With digital photography, you can film the audience in action at an earlier event and show them the results as part of your talk. Pros use this technique to inspire laughter, camaraderie, and spontaneity. Be the first on your management team to film or photograph the office staff hard at work and load it into your computer visuals. One fitness facility manager we know did just that to kick off his introduction at a staff retreat. They loved it. He also interviewed key supervisors and showed the interviews as part of the introduction.

People like hearing their names and seeing themselves in action. Will Rogers once said that the greatest sound to man was the sound of his own name correctly pronounced. It boosts self-esteem and motivates your listeners.

Audiences appreciate a creative approach to your topic. What if a wedding toast was given in a totally different way—for example, using an actual piece of toast, or as a group poem? What if the minister delivered the entire sermon as a responsive reading? What if the whole class gave the graduation address? Imagine the joy and fun of being in the audience for any of those events. Our creativity tends to wane the older we get. Give yours a second chance as you write your next presentation.

Your presentation is a gift that should hold some surprise.

24

Decide on Your Notes Policy

- **Using and not using notes are both professional approaches.**

- **Whatever you decide, be aware of any barriers between you and your audience.**

- **Never use a computer as your teleprompter—never!**

To speak well, you may need a note to remind you of key points—it's okay to use it, but don't read it. Don't allow notes to become a barrier between you and the audience. Talk show hosts use large note cards to prompt their memory. You can, also.

Utilize your notes but don't make a production out of them. Many professionals use cards with large type font on a table in front of the room to prompt their thinking. The audience may know the cards are present, but it is not a barrier. A slight glance and you will know where to go next. You may want a few traditional index cards with easy-to-read bullet points. You can carefully hold the cards in one hand, but don't play with them or shuffle them. Or you can place notes on a table or podium.

COACH'S COMMENTS

Your coach says: Whatever you do, be comfortable with your choice. The audience came to hear you, not critique you. If you use note cards, use them with aplomb and not apology. If you use sheets of paper, plan and practice how to hold them with ease and place them on the podium. If you select to read from the PowerPoint notes feature, that's fine, as long as you're well practiced. The types of notes you choose convey your personal style.

Some speakers use their PowerPoint slides as a guide. Take a slight glance and you are on your way. Never talk to the screen; focus only on your audience. The computer is deadly as a notes device. If you have ever seen a guest host on the television show *Saturday Night Live* look at his or her script on a teleprompter offstage you will recognize the problem. Your eye contact (see chapter 33) diminishes to nothing! Keep your computer screen away from your normal sight line or you will be tempted to read from it. The screen is a barrier! When we coach presenters, we often have them close their laptop so they can't see the screen at all. That way, they can't cheat!

Flipcharts (see chapter 35) can be great for notes. Write the notes on the side margin of the blank paper in light pencil. The audience will never see them, but you will. Even if they do, they will pay them no mind as long as you don't make a big deal out of it. You can also use Post-it notes to mark certain charts to turn to and you can number the notes for the correct order.

Memorize the outline of your talk, or even better—and this is what the pros do—memorize the three words that contain your entire point. That way you can constantly drive home your message. Look at some examples that are easy to remember, both for you and your listeners: "Now, not later," "Tomorrow's product today," "Win more customers," or "Perfect for performance."

When you give a eulogy, a sermon, or an award introduction, it is likely you will read more than normal because this is a special talk, not one easily remembered. The same rule applies—use the notes and the script, but don't make it look like it is the first time you have read it. The trick is to refer to the script, but not read it. This means you should practice often ahead of time, out loud, and in the setting, if possible.

Giving a eulogy? Arrive a few hours ahead of time and practice.

Giving an award? Especially practice the pronunciation of the names. Delivering a sermon in church? Rehearse, practice . . . and keep it short! Practice with the notes you intend to use. Often, you'll find that you'll want to change something—delete a line, add a phrase, or even change a story considerably. Also, practicing with the notes you intend to use allows you to feel their weight, their location, and their timing.

The audience came to hear your words; make sure you remember the point of your words.

25

Begin Unexpectedly— Involve Your Audience!

- **Audiences appreciate a unique approach.**
- **Rapport can become predictable.**
- **You can build a community of learners in only a few moments—if you invest the time.**

Send a message to your audience, from the start, that that meeting is going to be run differently—it is going to include them. Ask them for a "fun fact," an offbeat, more personal fact, an unusual detail about them as individuals. You can begin by telling your own. The more interesting your fun fact is, the better you will get the ball rolling for them and "break the ice" that so often plagues meetings at the beginning. We have heard serious businesspeople talk about being expert trampoline athletes in fourth grade, being career hippies (for a year!) in college, working at a penitentiary, herding sheep, and being arrested at age six! This one tremendously memorable activity gives you two things for your talk: an agenda and a rapport.

COACH'S COMMENTS

Your coach says: There are many other ways to begin unexpectedly without necessarily using the audience. What you want to be careful about here is to make your opening fit with what you are about to say. Your story should flow right into your message and your presentation. It is the "opening act" for the rest of what you are about to say. Never start with "I flew in from Chicago today

and . . ." or "I gotta tell you this great joke . . ." Both are death for
a presenter!

But what if you begin by walking away from the podium and
(with no other introduction) you say, "So I'm at my desk and . . ."
and you tell a story that bears directly on your topic? It can be funny,
but it doesn't have to be. It can be short, but need not be. It simply
must be interesting, different, and compelling.

Ask your audience for their "burning questions." To start
your audience brainstorming on their own burning question, ask
them this: "What do you want to learn the most at today's meeting? What question is burning at the forefront of your mind?"
When audience members tell you their burning questions, they
are creating an agenda for you—they are telling you what they
most want you to tell them. Their answers give you direction and
focus. When you ask a "What do you want?" question, you'll be
ordinary. When you use a "What is your burning question today?" approach, you will get their juices flowing!

If someone asked you for the one question you had about a
meeting, wouldn't you know precisely what you wanted answered? As the presenter, wouldn't you want to know what the
questions were ahead of time? Burning questions acquaint you
with the audience and their needs and become your agenda for
that presentation. Answer those questions and you will be a hit
with your audience.

Fun facts create instant rapport. We have been using the fun
fact for many years in our presentations to science and medical audiences. It is unexpected, provides a great way to relax the audience (and you!), and it allows for the audience members to connect
with one another. All those who fish, who fly-fish, or who fly-fish
with only a special kind of equipment can relate. Those who
bungee jump, who parachute, or who scuba dive will all quickly
get to know one another. And all those who won their second-
grade spelling bee will gather together at Table 3 for lunch!

Fun facts work best with audiences of less than twenty members. For larger audiences, break them into smaller groups of three

and ask for their burning questions and fun facts. Then take a few minutes to listen. Always write down the burning question on a flipchart. Always! It becomes your agenda for the meeting and shows them that you are interested in their goals as well as your own. Write down their answers word for word. Do not editorialize. It is OK to shorten what they said, but it is vital to use their precise words so there is no misunderstanding and no resentment. Write what they said and you will be perceived as a listener par excellence!

Always listen for any issue or question behind the question. If you hear it, ask. If they agree, write. If not, store it away for possible future use. Unexpected beginnings help the audience connect to you and to one another . . . and they tell you precisely what to say to best serve their needs.

26

End Unexpectedly

- **Avoid being too predictable, especially at the end.**
- **Use your creativity throughout your presentation, not only in the beginning.**
- **Develop your own signature story.**

How many times have you listened to a presenter who did not know how to end? Or one who ended his or her presentation with two or three (or more) endings? Some speakers say "in conclusion" or "finally" too many times before they are dragged off the stage. Some end abruptly with "that's it, any questions?"

Any time you neglect your ending, you cheat the audience of a rich conclusion that will help them remember what you said. Consider these alternatives instead:

- Ask for volunteers to say what they learned and what they will do differently. Then end with: "Here are three things I learned from all of you today."

- "Today we covered three simple and vital concepts . . ."

- "We have time for Q&A now. However, I do have a question I'd like each of you to consider as we leave here today . . ."

- "Let me close today by reviewing with you the burning questions [see chapter 25] we began with. What did we say about the first one . . . ? The second one . . . ?"

- You can also end with what is known as a "signature story."

A **"signature story" is a standard story many professional speakers will use often.** Some have two or three they will select from, but within these stories is the wisdom they want to impart on the audience. Some are funny, some are tearjerkers, some are motivational, and some have quick, punchy endings, but the signature story always has a unique, personal touch.

Kevin tries to use a "first impression" story whenever he can. "I met Ralph last week at the home office and as we sat down . . ." This is a highly specific, one-time signature story. It is powerful, but it doesn't need to be the only signature story you tell. Kevin also uses five generic signature stories that relate to follow-up, change, leadership, working with others, and personal development. Sometimes when he speaks for the second time to a group, audience members will come up ahead of time and say, "Are you going to tell the 'river otter' story again? I hope you will." Others will accost him after the talk with "why didn't you tell the 'cane' story?" Like children, adults love stories and they love to have them repeated.

Two things to remember about signature stories: first, although personal to you, they must be audience-driven (or they will be boring and disappointing); and second, they must be rehearsed and practiced. As we have advised you to spend time on your first four minutes (see chapter 12), we also strongly suggest you have your ending down cold! It is the audience's last impression of you.

Just a routine business update, you say? While a signature story may be awkward here, a story, personal event, or short quote may not be. For example, if you're a personnel director giving current hiring statistics for the company, you can end with a summary of why recent hires say they like to work for the company. If you're a marketing manager hyping a product, you can end by passing out samples of the product with a customer quote on the PowerPoint. You will enhance your impact if you end unexpectedly.

COACH'S COMMENTS

Your coach says: The problem with telling the audience you will be finishing soon is that the audience takes that as a sign you *are* finished, and they mentally go somewhere else. In short, they finish before you do. When you end, do so with a flair, but end. And remember, ending unexpectedly does not mean ending abruptly. One final piece of advice: Always end on the minute for a short talk and five minutes early for a long one. The audience and the planner will love you for it.

Leave your audience with something of lasting value, and they will perceive you to be of value to them.

27

Face a Trend with an Antitrend

- **People listen best to something new or different.**
- **For every trend, there is an antitrend.**
- **Antitrends are more interesting than trends.**

If you're looking for a new approach to your next talk, you can gain attention with trends. You can also capture attention with antitrends. An antitrend exists for every possible trend, and it represents the opposite. For example, the more high-tech we become, the more personal contact we need. In professional speaking, this antitrend is represented by a gradual move away from PowerPoint slides and back to the podium. The larger we get, the smaller we get. Housing trends have shifted from five-bedroom homes to empty nesters' condos. The older we get, the younger we become. Those same empty nesters are also extremely interested in health and appearance. Audiences pay attention when a speaker talks about trends and antitrends.

Do research to discover the trends in your field. The Internet has thousands of trends-related sites. Your payoff will be seeing people's eyes light up when you mention the word "trend." Trends are appealing because they strike interest in the unknown and the unexplored. Why leave them to the marketing department or to the journalists? We can all benefit! Author Faith Popcorn discovered this years ago as she wrote her bestselling books on trends and how they affect everyday life. She coined the term "cocooning" based on the trend to stay at home for fun and relaxation.

Read daily papers and magazines to stay abreast of trends.

You'll see them everywhere. Fashion provides many examples. Any time blue jeans come to the forefront, so do opposites like fur or the color black or pearls. As we write this book, the "trendy" wear their jeans with a tailored, classy jacket and pearls. There is currently a reversal from low-carb diets back toward low-fat diets. Other trends are healthy fast-food options for kids, hybrid car/trucks, and comfortable hotel beds in a reviving travel industry. These general trends provide useful ideas for comparisons, analogies, documentation of public habits, and other supplements for your talk.

Tie the trend into your topic. To make trends meaningful, you can cite trends directly related to your field. Watch how topics are repeated in your professional journals and e-mails. Attend conferences and be alert to the most frequently addressed topics. In professional speaking, the trend toward marketing with an e-zine was easy to pick up on after a few months of professional research and development.

Don't forget the antitrends! They grab attention, too. In the midst of the e-learning (electronic learning) trend in the training and development field, Cyndi coauthored a book entitled *Training from the Heart.* Thanks to the clever eye of her acquisitions editor, the book immediately grabbed professional trainers' attention because it focused on face-to-face communication in the midst of new distance technology. Of course, there were also bestselling e-learning books at that time, but the phenomenon of the antitrend is that it exists peaceably alongside of the trend. And it is even more interesting.

Discover an antitrend that will help sell your idea. A recent news article noticed that some restaurants were reinstalling phone booths (sans hookups) as quiet places for cell phone users to make calls. For anyone who's ever been a victim of another cell phone user's conversation in a public place, this idea makes sense. If you spoke on the lack of privacy in today's world, this would be a perfect example. It also fits many other topics: business etiquette, time management, work/life balance, technology, use of space, or restaurant design.

COACH'S COMMENTS

Question: I like this idea of using an antitrend, but I don't have a lot of time to research what they are. Any ideas?

Your coach says: How about creatively suggesting what they are? It's easier to find a list of trends than a list of antitrends. Find a list of trends and then select some that make sense to use in your talk. For example, if the real trend is toward weight loss, you could argue for an antitrend toward extreme chocolate desserts. If the real trend is toward falling interest rates, you could document an antitrend toward low-priced condos for some markets.

You can suggest an antitrend of your own. Market it as part of your talk. Consider a "to don't" list as opposed to a "to do" list. How about suggesting a sales sampler instead of a sales survey? What if people guessed instead of researched to find the right answer? Suppose a typically casual group turns formal for a time? While these ideas may sound unusual, they'll certainly invite listening. To manage time, a sales trainer we know says "no" to the good and "yes" to the great. Many articles are written on "ten ways not to do . . ." just about anything—buy a house, raise a teenager, clean a bathroom, or stay happily married.

Use the rule of three when you talk about trends. Trends catch eyes and ears because they're new and different. Don't belabor them. Talk of no more than three at a time. Three fascinating trends are more meaningful to the listener than ten. If you have ten trends in your industry, then highlight three and provide background information for the others.

A speaker who cites trends and antitrends grabs instant attention.

Part V

Create a Connection

28

Start with the First Step

- **Connect and include your audience.**
- **Clear agenda items help orient the audience to you.**
- **Opening moments are important.**

Adults want two things when they settle into a room for a seminar or a speech. They want to feel connected and included. In traditional meetings, this need is ignored and presenters jump right into the material. Don't make this mistake. When participants feel well taken care of, they learn more, cooperate more, remember more, and give the meeting higher ratings!

Where do you prefer to socialize? At a home where the door is left open, you hang up your own coat, and find someone—anyone—to talk with? Or is it more likely you'd rather visit a home where someone greets you warmly at the door and introduces you to the other guests? It is no different at corporate meetings.

> **COACH'S COMMENTS**
> **Your coach says:** Often the first step is the hardest. Would you rather push a car that was already moving, or get it moving by yourself from a dead stop? That's how it works with your presentation skills. Whatever you do, begin. Even if it is a small step forward—just begin.

Here's how to welcome your participants "at the door." Set a positive, more comfortable tone with your introductions and opening. Be enthusiastic, but maintain your calm as you begin.

Clearly set out the agenda and the overall goals of the meeting or, at least, your own presentation's goals. Make sure you introduce (and thank) key participants and define their role in the group.

Opening moments are important. Just as a horse can sense if you are a good rider, so too can an audience sense that either all is well, or they are in for trouble. They do all of this in the first four minutes of your presentation. Many times it has little to do with the words you are saying; more often it has to do with how you are acting, walking, and conducting yourself. If you want to be an excellent speaker, do one thing—rehearse those first four minutes!

An audience who feels welcome and included will work harder to reach positive outcomes under the guidance of their host—you, the speaker.

THREE WAYS
Three Tips for the Moment Before You Stand Up:
- Take a deep breath from the diaphragm.

- Sip from a glass of water without ice.

- Smile at your tablemates or coworkers.

Three Things to Do Right After You Sit Down:
- Take a deep breath from the diaphragm.

- Sip from a glass of water without ice.

- Smile at your tablemates or coworkers!

(Yes, these two should look familiar!)

29

Try a Three-Part Warm-up

- **Warm up the participants to you.**
- **Warm up the participants to each other.**
- **Warm up the participants to the topic.**

Imagine you've just attended a wedding. You've come alone. Now you find yourself at the cocktail reception before dinner, chatting with the stranger standing next to you. You both agree that it was a lovely wedding. The bride was beautiful. The groom was appropriately nervous. You spend the next forty-five minutes being as interesting and as charming as it is humanly possible for you to be. You have pulled out your business card and all the stops. Finally, there is nothing left for you to say.

Suddenly, the doors to the dining room open, and you both reach into your pockets for your table assignment cards. Surprise! You are both at Table 19. Summoning your energy, you realize the conversational evening has just begun.

Facing the opening of a long presentation is similar in many ways. You need to be personable and dynamic and engaging, yet you are also responsible for building a lasting connection for the entire program. Consider these three starting strategies to help you establish and keep the connection you want: Warm up the participants to you, to each other, and to the topic.

Warm up the participants to you. Aristotle talked about achieving ethos with an audience. Ethos is accomplished through a presenter's dynamism, competence, and trustworthiness. Dynamism can be communicated through vocal and body energy and thorough practice of your wording and delivery.

Competence is sometimes harder to communicate immediately. An idea for quickly establishing competence is to creatively reference your research in your opening remarks. For example, for a presentation on effective employee orientations, you could ask the group to think of you as Jane (or Joe) Newcomer, a new person in their department, adding, "I'm one of eighty thousand Americans right now starting my first day on the job." Continuing with workforce statistics from the viewpoint of J. Newcomer then stimulates audience interest.

A way to achieve trustworthiness early on is to sincerely relate to the audience's situation. When participants feel you are one of them, you achieve "an assimilation effect." Whether it's relating to their work or lack of it, you can build on and assimilate their experience. A career day presenter can refer to the fact that we all had a first job. Everyone can relate to that!

Warm up the participants to each other. Have you ever been to a speech or seminar where you weren't warmed up at the beginning? Most likely, it got off to a slow start. Perhaps you don't know how to warm up a crowd or have agonized over what sort of warm-up to select. Partner or self-introductions with an expectation or challenge related to the topic are not necessarily the most creative choices, but, happily, they always work. Here are some choices that are fun, but a bit more risky: 1. Share three things about yourself—one being false. 2. Share an accomplishment you're proud of. 3. Share something very few people know about you.

Warm up participants to the topic. You can creatively reference the topic by asking participants to share a recent occurrence with respect to the topic, a recent success related to the topic, or how they would prioritize the topic in their work lives on a scale of one to ten and why. For example, if you're presenting on the current economic situation, it's easy to get a quick one-to-ten scale and show of hands on how people are affected by it (ten: strongly affected, one: not affected at all).

COACH'S COMMENTS

Question: This warm-up idea is never done in my company. I'd like to try it. Are you sure it works?

Your coach says: Asking an audience to do anything for the first time—especially a warm-up activity—can be scary. When the crowd is large and unknown, it is difficult to muster the courage to let go of the podium and allow them to interact. Try to remember that the audience will appreciate the break and will feel better when they do connect with another audience member, even if it's just to say hello.

When the group is small and very well known, the same strategy applies. In this case, since they know one another, ask them to turn to the person next to them and rate their day on a scale of one to ten. Laughter will usually result and people will begin talking about their day without being asked. This begins with a bit of courage on your part and a large dose of caring for your audience. The pros know the value of the warm-up; it makes life easier for them in the long run.

Include all three warm-up parts in your opening moments for an instant connection to your audience.

FROM THE RANKS

"I learned my biggest lesson in how to warm up an audience while in traffic school. I had made an illegal right turn on red. I was sitting in the back row with a bad attitude when the traffic school presenter walked in and announced, 'I'm not a police officer; I've taught driver's education for twenty-five years, and I'm an ordinary driver just like you.' And then she said, 'We'll go around the room, and will everyone please say your first name and why you're here?' You can imagine my reluctance, but the people in the front row played along as did everyone, and by the time it was my turn, I clearly declared, 'Beverly Jameson. Right on red!' She was a master at connecting!"

—Beverly, mortgage consultant

30

Connect with a Grieving Audience

- **Find connections in the past.**
- **Tell simple stories with perfectly stunning quotes.**
- **Discover and bring out the poet in you.**
- **Unify around a theme for maximum impact.**

Drew's memorial service was filled with tributes from those who knew him well. Drew died at age forty-one after battling a difficult disease. On a sunny autumn afternoon in a suburban church in his hometown, the friends he went to high school with and the neighbors he grew up among took time to remember their friend. Many of them came forward to speak throughout the hour-long service, which was hosted by a friend of the family. The minister in attendance delivered only the closing prayer.

Drew loved the arts and spent most of his time working with the arts. He graduated from an academy of merchandising design. He performed in school plays in his youth and designed window displays professionally during his short adult life. Those memorializing Drew shared beautiful, emotional connections to his artistic life. It was a service born more of caring and love than professional skill at the podium—typical of memorial services held around the world hosted by loving, inexperienced presenters who somehow always rise to the task.

Like those neighbors and friends, you may be asked at some point in your life to memorialize someone or celebrate an occasion with your words in front of a large group. This type of occasion allows perhaps the most natural suitable time to connect with emotions. Psychologist Alfred Adler once said, "Emotions are like the gas in our tank. They don't drive the car, but they provide the fuel to move." You can find the fuel to move your presentation in a variety of ways, but mostly in your preplanning.

COACH'S COMMENTS

Question: Help! I've been asked to say a few words at my brother-in-law's funeral along with some others who knew him well. They want us to tell a story. Any advice?

Your coach says: This is not an unusual request. It personalizes the ceremony and is healing for the audience. Be glad to be a part of it. Be yourself; raise your volume level and look the audience in the eye. You may want to share some way that your brother-in-law changed your life in an ordinary way; perhaps he helped you pick out your first used car, or rescued you from a blowout on the highway before you understood car maintenance. Grieving audiences love to hear simple stories that aren't too long or too sad.

The first step to finding emotional connections is to look back. Find the old scrapbooks and discover ways to tie yesterday to today. One of Drew's neighbors, now in her fifties, found photos of all of Drew's plays that she had attended when she had been a young mother. They reminded her of all the cast parties when she brought food to the excited teen performers. Her eulogy began as a simple recitation of "stage-neighbor" memories. Her closing words connected beautifully to the audience: "Drew is in heaven now—where the arts have to be the ultimate!" She looked out at the audience for a few moments, smiled, and sat down.

Another way to connect emotionally is to conduct telephone interviews with people who are acquainted with the person or situation. Using others' quotes will lend you credibility and variety. That way, you don't have to be so conscious of coming up with every little witty thing yourself. This worked perfectly for Drew's mother, whose eulogy was perhaps the most tearful. The audience empathized with the unkind turnaround of the way things are supposed to be—losing a child before one's own death. Her words held gentle memories and thank-yous, but the audience was able to laugh with her when she included a quote from her six-year-old granddaughter. The little girl, upon hearing a careful explanation of her uncle's death, thought for a moment and said, "Oh, I see. Today I graduated from kindergarten and Uncle Drew graduated from life."

As you plan your remarks, discover the poet in you! Remember how your English teachers encouraged you to use colorful words and poetic imagery? Drew's high school drama teacher employed alliteration to make a point: "Drew believed in faith, family, and friends." He followed that with a timeless quote from the funeral service in Thornton Wilder's play *Our Town*. "Something's eternal and that something has to do with human beings." After that, he shared his own philosophy, which was poetic in itself: "In order to heal, we must be ourselves." His key to connecting was poetry.

Develop a theme as you build your connection. In Drew's service, perhaps the most memorable tribute came from his best friend, Traci, now a successful wine expert in a large city. Traci quoted from letters Drew had sent her from the time he was in high school and throughout his adult life. A great interpreter, she read his words with honest energy and emotion and not a little theatrical talent. Through the letters, the audience lived Drew's self-doubts, joys, and plans. It became clear the theme in Drew's life was fun, partnered with artistic spontaneity. Traci's key to connection was her love for her friend, evident in her careful development of the theme through his letters.

Unity, lyricism, poetry, and love—these are ingredients that the occasional presenter can bring to any opportunity where an emotional connection with the audience is demanded. They are useful not just in eulogy situations, but also for award banquets, weddings, christenings, and graduations. Because they connect to the heart, these talks don't need to be perfectly smooth or practiced. What's most important is that they are real.

To connect emotionally is to be real and anchored in unity, lyricism, poetry, and love.

Connect via Stories and More

- **Within every story lies a lesson.**
- **Stories connect head to heart.**
- **A story drops anchor—anywhere you want.**

Make the stories your own. Kevin was coaching an oncologist/
hematologist on his speaking skills one day. It was just Kevin, the
doctor, and the videographer who was recording the speech seg-
ments on video for replay later. As they were finishing lunch in
this small conference room, the videographer asked Kevin for ten
minutes to "go outside for a moment." As Kevin nodded "yes,"
the physician looked up from his salad and said point-blank to
the young videographer, "You're going out for a smoke, aren't
you?" Somewhat startled, the young man sheepishly said, "Yes,
I am. I want to quit, but you know."

The physician leaned forward and said, "Why not make today
the day? I will teach you how to quit today." He then went into an
extensive description of nicotine and its effect on the body, the cel-
lular structure, even how the tobacco companies work to deliver
even more nicotine through the use of ammonia on the leaves.
"Actually, cigarettes should be called 'nicotine delivery systems'
for what they really do," he said quietly.

Then he added a remarkable statement in an almost pastoral
way reminiscent of a priest, minister, or rabbi: "I admire your
courage. What you are about to embark upon takes a great deal of
courage, and I just want you to know I am behind you and I admire you for it. Actually, quitting cigarettes is more difficult than

quitting cocaine or heroin. Cigarettes are much, much more addictive." The videographer took a long glance, gulped, and then said, "You know, Doc, you are right. It was much easier for me to quit cocaine and heroin!"

This doctor connected with a story about tobacco and the human body. He seized an opportunity, an unexpected one at that. He used a time-tested technique—he leaned forward and spoke with concern and compassion. Finally, he engaged in a conversation with this young man without judgment.

Look around you. You can do the same. Stories are all around you—the dog you adopted, your daughter's first time driving, the struggling yellow rose in your garden, your oldest goldfish, and any one of a hundred "stories" that fill our lives. Cyndi developed an entire talk once by sitting in her garden. The flowers began to take on the personalities of people and before she knew it, she had the sturdy lily, the pouty carnation, the finicky rose, and the independent iris likened to coworkers on the job.

COACH'S COMMENTS

Your coach says: Professionals collect stories and you can, too. Watch service (especially good service) at restaurants, talk to taxi drivers (you will hear the funniest stories), read some magazine completely out of your field regularly, interview service workers, or learn a new language. All these methods will offer you a wealth of stories that may or may not be useful. Remember to try them out in casual conversation like professional comedians do so you know if they are interesting. Then change a bit here and there and see what the reaction is. Stories are compelling and irresistible to audiences. Your stories are your gold; they represent your pain, your experience, your wins and losses. They also unite. Think of all the things people share: everyone has a weird relative, an annoying neighbor, and a funny wedding story. You do too. Use it!

Stories can spring from the simplest things. If you feel connected to something—an event, a moment, or a person—there is most likely a story to tell. A pro we know has a memorable story focusing on her father smoking a pipe in an easy chair. Another tells a hilarious tale of an ill-fitting seat belt on the plane. Still another captivates her audiences with tales about raising her troubled teenage son to success. The more people can connect—the better. When the Mt. Everest climber tells his story, it works best when he connects to the audience's everyday challenges that seem equally insurmountable.

If you know your audience, you're a step ahead. Priests, rabbis, and ministers spend their entire career speaking at funerals about people they have only known in death. Although their sermons may be "standard and generic," they do have to personalize them with some knowledge of the person who died. The smart ones interview the experts—the family members—at the wake. One priest gave a very generic homily and then said, "I didn't know Dorothy, but her family tells me she was a dignified woman who liked a good cigar! I really do wish I had known you, Dorothy," he said as he looked at the casket. It brought down the house! Too bad he didn't start his homily with that line!

Another minister simply asks a question: "How many of you . . . ?" and his audience begins to smile and nod in agreement because they know he knows. What if you began your next presentation or started a content section inside your talk with a short focused story? Be careful not to get so excited about your story that you go on and on. When you use the story as an example or a metaphor, you will capture the lived experience of the audience and you'll see smiles, nods, and connections.

Adults and children have one thing in common—both love and are entranced by stories.

FROM THE RANKS

"In talking about how important teachers are to their students' achievement, I told my staff that as a young girl on a farm, I had very literally watched corn grow. As a cultivator goes through the rows in the spring, occasionally a small cornstalk gets bent over and weighed down by soil. As the stalk continues to grow there comes a moment when the stalk is strong enough to right itself and literally flip the dirt from its leaves. Then the leaves slowly uncurl to receive the rays. Similarly, with the light from a caring teacher, students can right themselves and come into their full stature. Months later I received a call from one of the teachers saying, 'Leslie, I saw it. You are right; it is beautiful.' She then told me she had driven into the country to watch corn grow."

—Leslie, secondary school administrator

No Joke! Know the Risks

- **Jokes on you are the best.**
- **Jokes on others are the worst.**
- **Humor works better than jokes.**

Actor and entrepreneur Paul Newman once said, "There are three rules to running a business. And I don't know any of them." This type of humor works well in a presentation because it sets up a serious expectation and then surprises. It's not a joke that offends. In fact, it is self-deprecating. Audiences love self-deprecating humor, especially when the speaker is someone who has earned their respect in other ways. People love to laugh at others' mistakes and, mostly, they love to laugh in a clean way.

Any presentation, even a eulogy, can benefit from humor. Similar to nearly everything else involved in a successful presentation, humor can be preplanned. Granted, spontaneous humor is perhaps the funniest, but preplanned humor is respectable and endearing. Some speakers are just better impromptu humorists, but every speaker can learn to plan ahead.

Think about your audience's world. Relate to the jargon. Most of us can laugh at the jargon we use in our field—the mysterious terminology we've learned that others outside the field don't know. For example, we speakers talk about platform skills, product innovation, and bureau holds and bookings. Every profession has expert jargon. You can poke fun here. Cyndi once addressed construction specifications engineers—people who know more about paint toxins and mold than anyone else in the world. In her opening, she acknowledged her respect for their work, adding that, before speaking to them, she wanted to do her homework to get a perspective on toxic paint and mold. So, she went to the basement and stood awhile in her teenage son's room. Anyone who has or has ever been a teenager could relate to the typical state of a teenage boy's room!

Kevin spoke to a group of leading electric garage door engineers and decided not to make any jokes or humorous comments despite his desire to do so. Instead, he simply responded to the humor they gave him when he solicited answers to questions he threw out to the audience. Kevin didn't think what they said was "that funny," but the audience thought it was hysterical. They knew their business better. (And who says engineers aren't funny beyond words!)

Find common ground that makes everyone laugh. Everyone has difficult days, annoying service experiences, less than friendly neighbors, least favorite relatives, and peculiar habits. These issues put people in a common circle. Ask your contact if there are particular challenges in the area of work/life balance or commuting or change that you can relate to in a humorous way.

Avoid old traps. Jokes are very personal. When performed by professionals like Steve Martin, Jay Leno, Jerry Seinfeld, or even the aging but still performing Don Rickles, they work because the delivery is superb and the fun or ridicule is expected. When performed by you and us, they are extremely risky. First of all, your chances of hitting an audience with a new joke are very slim. Internet jokes move at an amazing pace; new jokes become old quickly. Cyndi's husband was surprised to receive an e-mailed joke from his boss about a bad-mouthed parrot who learned a lesson in the freezer. The joke itself was hilarious but he had heard it first two years ago! Listen to your friends try telling a joke they heard and watch the reaction of others who are listening. Not everyone gets it, not everyone laughs heartily, and not everyone appreciates the joke. Now multiply that by a room full of people looking directly at you! Jokes are dangerous territory unless you have a staff of writers, a late-night show, and an ego the size of Texas!

COACH'S COMMENTS

Your coach says: If you are a presenter, tell jokes only when you are with those who love you or at the bar when everyone, including you, is feeling very loose and forgiving. Never anywhere else. Never. Good humor brings people together; it never alienates them. We laugh at pain we have in common. If, as a presenter, you don't have the pain in common (job loss, bad boss, difficult child, weight gain), then you absolutely cannot attempt humor in that area.

Watch the potty humor. Any semblance of reference to elimination is risky. One esteemed manager once referred to his team being in "deep doggy doo-doo" if they didn't turn around. What did that choice say about him? It certainly wasn't mature. When you are the boss no one is going to tell you that you messed up, but they will feel it. The same holds true with any audience. Few will tell you the truth. You must know the truth before you open your mouth.

Recognize the obvious. Image consultants tell us that nearly every speaker at their AICI (Association of Image Consultants International) conferences makes the same type of reference to his or her image—how appearing in front of image consultants is intimidating with respect to suit and tie or shoe selection. It's not at all original to mention this. Similarly, nonprofessional speakers often mention their nervousness when addressing a National Speakers Association conference of ours. We've heard it all before. Cyndi once spoke to endodontists (root canal specialists) who told her they had heard every root canal joke imaginable. Be careful and ask first. Always interview several audience members prior to your talk even if they are your coworkers. You will learn more in those few moments than any PowerPoint tweaking or Internet search can provide. There is always a risk in the obvious that is all too often not so obvious to you.

Beware of sex, ethnicity, politics, and gender jokes. Stay far away from anything that would harm your credibility and reputation here. We recently watched an esteemed elderly speaker fall into the trap of telling a dated joke about blondes. While a fairly innocent joke, there were many women in the room who commented on their feedback forms about it. You cannot poke fun at any group unless you are a member of it. And even then, you have to be careful. Humor is great but it has its time and place. Work instead to be interesting, valuable, and innovative in your presentation.

Always ask and practice first. If you use humor, try it out on someone. Ask your husband, an actor or performer friend, a high school speech team coach, a minister—anyone who may have a good idea or two. Try it out on a trusted coworker or coach or college friend. If you or they feel it is in the least bit risky, ask your contact or meeting planner for a vote. E-mail them the script. Some cultures allow a lot more humor than others. We are often able to insert executives' names into funny examples in our programs, but we always ask first.

Bill Brooks is an experienced speaker and former football coach. He is a man's man, big, fun, very knowledgeable, and a great off-the-cuff speaker. His advice serves us all well: "When in doubt, drop it. Never risk offending."

Humor is best when it builds common ground.

33

Practice Consistent Eye Contact

- **Your eyes and theirs are key to your message making sense to them.**
- **Be personal even to large audiences.**
- **Learning happens "one to one."**

Use eye contact wisely. In four-to-five-second bursts, make sure you make eye contact with everyone. Begin with a friendly face in the audience and then move to the next one. This will help anchor you and alleviate your nervousness, too. As you proceed, finish a thought with eye contact and make sure you only use one message per set of eyes. It takes us several seconds (seven to ten) to complete a thought, so try to complete a thought with each person you look at.

COACH'S COMMENTS

Your coach says: This is a developed habit and skill, and an important one. If you are not very good at it, observe it first in others. Watch how they do or do not establish and maintain eye contact with you. Then experiment with strangers . . . you'll never see them again! Then work at it some each day. Successful people have this one trait in common . . . and so can you.

Speaking is really a one-to-one sport. Professional speaker and author Marjorie Brody calls it "an audience-centered sport" and we agree. Although you may be addressing five hundred, you are really speaking to each one. Your eyes convey this.

Watch your favorite announcers on any busy news program, like *CNN Headline News*. They excel at using their eyes for impact. Looking straight into the camera, they punctuate the words of the text with their eyes. Who else do you know with great eye contact? Who do you know who uses their eyes for positive impact?

The late Cardinal Bernardin from Chicago once remarked that eye contact is a sign of real connection, real intimacy. It sounds clichéd, but eyes truly are the "windows to the soul," to the extent that it's difficult for eyes to lie. Pay attention to this in your daily life.

Over the period of two semesters while teaching at Loyola University in Chicago, Kevin watched how students used their eyes for impact in his classes. During small group discussions, the students who utilized their time the best and made their point most effectively often looked the others in the eye, and also used their eyes to punctuate what they said. They looked at the other students, not just their professor.

If eyes "speak volumes" (and they do), make sure your eyes speak the volumes you want emphasized.

FROM THE PROS

"What I have learned is that even when the verbal communication is going one way (as in a keynote), there is still communication from the audience. Making strong eye contact with the audience allows the speaker to 'hear' what they are telling you. Puzzled looks? Acknowledge, and perhaps give another example of your point. People scribbling furiously? Slow down, pause, or let them know there are handouts at the end. Nods and smiles? You've got them. They are listening and into whatever you are talking about. And if you as the speaker are feeling unsure, find a friendly face and speak directly to that person for a sentence or two. You will feel your confidence refresh."

—Jerilyn, organizational development specialist

34

Use Your Introduction to Connect

- **It can establish your persona.**
- **It can link you to the topic.**
- **It can build your credibility quietly.**

You have a great opportunity to advance both your character and ideas in the manner in which you are introduced. Even when you write and deliver your own introduction, you can accomplish a lot in a few minutes. You can be straightforward and factual or funny and unexpected in what you choose to say about yourself and your topic. It's important to have some type of planned introduction, even if you're presenting to the same team you present to every month.

Create a mood. Even at the mundane monthly meeting, you can establish a tone with your introduction. Consider the difference between, "Well, here we are again with the monthly update," and "Friends and salespeople of excellence, wait until you hear the numbers this month." Or, if you need to refer to your name and position, consider the difference between, "I'm Joe, IT manager," and "Good morning. I'm Joe Brown, the IT manager on fifth floor for the last five years. I'm happy to be among all of you on third floor as I've often wondered what really goes on down here. Seriously, you are doing great work in Internet marketing and I'm pleased to update you with this system information today." Which approaches show warmth and creativity? Which show little to no preplanning? Audiences make a quick first impression, and what you choose to say first is lasting.

Establish your expertise. Take your moment in the spotlight to shine. You can do it very factually or in a more subtle manner. You can say, "I'm Char Stewart and I have over twenty years of experience in training and development," or instead, "In the last twenty years, I've seen our training methods of delivery change from flipcharts to e-learning and now back to flipcharts! Who would have known?" You can relate to the audience's experience and tie yours in; for example, "While most of you have lots of experience with this drug, I have more experience with its predecessor. In fact, I hope to be able to compare notes throughout this presentation."

Coach your introducer. If someone else is introducing you, do what a professional speaker does. A pro sends the introduction in advance, has a copy of it in 14-point font, and gives the introducer specific instructions about any important points. While this may sound egotistical, it's not at all. It's very client-focused and in tune with doing the prework. The introduction is a crucial vehicle for setting the tone of your presentation and the tone of you. The more careful you are about this, the better.

COACH'S COMMENTS

Your coach says: Even when you are short of time, don't neglect prework. Sending an e-mail to say you are coming to the meeting is better than nothing. Interviews are best but are not always possible. Make some connection, if only by voice mail. If you're strapped for time, you can call when you know no one will answer, after business hours or early in the morning. Simply leave the message in an upbeat tone, mention the meeting you're looking forward to meeting them at, and your contact information. They don't call back, but when they meet they usually thank you for the call!

We've learned from experience how important this is and what a difference it makes. Once, for an after-dinner speech, Cyndi had faxed her introduction and also brought it along, double spaced in 14-point font, to give to the introducer upon arrival. However, just before the introducer began, she nervously dropped it, failed to quiet down the loud after-dinner crowd, and read it in a rote monotone. Though Cyndi had written it humorously, no one heard it but three other people in front. In retrospect, Cyndi learned she should have alerted her introducer to the importance of the tone, especially in an after-dinner format.

Most people are not introduced at length in a typical business or social presentation, but most people are introduced in some way, however briefly. Someone usually says, "Here's Joe to talk about the weekly sales predictions," or "We're happy to have Sandy here from IT to tell us about the new firewall." It only takes a moment to ask your introducer to use a specific phrase to set you up with humor or a relevant credential to help you connect. For example, "Joe, who's always in the know, is ready to share what he knows . . ." or "Sandy, who puts out fires with the firewall." Don't be shy about asking the contact that will introduce you to use a special phrase to solidify your goal. You can write it down for them so they don't forget.

Time spent on a fitting introduction creates a connection.

THREE WAYS TO PREPARE

- Do you know the three things the meeting planner wants?

- Do you know the three things this audience needs from you?

- Do you know the three things you most want to impart?

If you know all nine, you will be ready. If not, call until you know.

FROM THE RANKS

"The thing I keep learning when I am speaking is that people like to be part of the process. They like it when they are asked questions or to complete sentences or are polled about how they feel about something."

—Pat, director of business development

35

Connect with Visual Simplicity

- **A flipchart is a classic tool for connection.**
- **Slides are meant to support you—not to steal attention from you.**
- **The audience came to see you, not your slides.**

Use a flipchart as an excellent supplement to your moderating and informing. Flipcharts involve your audience naturally because the audience watches and waits for you to write, to teach, and to involve them. For all those in your audience who are visually oriented or easily distracted, the flipchart can be a visual marker or reminder of what is being talked about. Consider using the simple, primitive, lonely flipchart as a coteacher.

When you write on the flipchart, do not write and talk at the same time. If you face the flipchart and speak, they will not hear you. Know what you are going to write, write it down, and then turn and talk to your audience. Even this brief silence allows the audience to pay even more attention to what you are writing and to what you are about to say.

Use a flipchart to record the burning questions, but be sure you understand each question before you begin writing. If you do not get it, ask them to say more so that you understand and can write down the point succinctly. Write with their words, not yours. Be very careful when you summarize what they said. Look for the "head nod." If you don't get their agreement, ask again. If they are unsure, ask the audience. There is always someone who does understand and can put it into words. Don't hurry here. You are building trust and rapport with your audience.

COACH'S COMMENTS

Your coach says: Work for simplicity here. Think connective-ness not impressiveness. One compelling word on the screen is better than twenty. Avoid reproducing cartoons from *The New Yorker* or *The Far Side*. Every amateur does it, no one can read the caption, and it is usually funny only to the presenter and those in the front row! Also, it is very illegal to use a cartoon without copyright permission, except in educational, not-for-profit settings. Remember, your visuals are only aids. The audience came to see you—not your slides. Some of the best presentations have been done with no visuals whatsoever. Using only a flipchart works too. Think connection.

If you are speaking and someone else is recording the information, repeat what you understood the audience member to have said so that the recorder knows what to write. If you are recording, write so that the person in the back row can see it without squinting. Don't use a red marker because it's harder to see. Black and blue are best. Test the markers before you begin; they're often dry or the wrong kind. Dry erase markers aren't as easy to see as regular flipchart markers and hotels often make this mistake in the setup.

If the discussion during the meeting relates to one of the burning questions the group asked earlier, direct the group's attention to the flipchart and see if the discussion has satisfied those who had that particular burning question, or if there are additional questions relating to it. The flipchart can also summarize all the points of view in a discussion. This visual example lets the audience know there can be many answers or views.

The flipchart often offers more flexibility and creativity than a PowerPoint presentation. It requires no electricity, it allows you and the audience to move from one concept to another on the spot, and it gives the audience a feel for your taking their needs into account, not just your prepared presentation.

Slides, on the other hand, require you to build a foundation with your audience before you launch into detailed slide presentations. Be flexible with the slides and slide sets used. Don't cling too tightly to the slide deck provided or there will be no time for discussion or facilitation. One way to facilitate discussions is to have a slide that specifically invites interaction. This keeps you on track and tells the audience it is their turn. Another technique not used as frequently as it should be involves inserting summary slides throughout your presentation. This allows for more learning, audience alignment with you, and a very effective way to teach your main points.

A keypad voting system now used in many corporate meetings can be an excellent evaluation tool after a meeting. In keypad voting, each attendee has a device that allows them to vote. Their votes are then automatically tallied and displayed on the screen in real time by a keypad technician. This system can "review" the day's materials and be supplemented with key questions about future ideas for each topic.

For evaluation purposes, questions and multiple-choice answers can be created about how useful the meeting was, how well the participants liked the format, how the meeting compared to others, and how they liked the keypad system. While paper evaluations aren't tabulated until the meeting is over and the participants gone, keypad voting is quick, easy, and provides immediate feedback for everyone.

Many technical presentations to physicians, engineers, and attorneys use keypad voting throughout the presentation in order to stimulate discussion and to show diversity. While you do not have to take care of the technology yourself, it is important to be familiar with the technology and how you will use it. Make the keypad technician your "best friend" prior to your talk and things will flow much easier!

**Visuals do more than display information—
they help you connect with your audience.**

FROM THE PROS

"If I get a good answer from someone in the audience, I throw them a Payday candy bar (because everyone loves a good Payday). It got to be that when I didn't do it, people complained!"

—Caryn, author and marketing specialist

36

Connect with Visual Innovation

- **Visuals don't have to be electronic.**
- **"Nonvisuals" spark creativity.**

How often do you think of visuals and immediately think of Power-Point slides? These are certainly helpful, no doubt, but don't limit yourself—and don't limit your audience. Dare to be different! What can you do with a prop, a flipchart, an object, or even an "invisible word"?

One of Kevin's fellow professors had his flipchart and his lecture all ready for his graduate students one day. All was in order. Then, as he opened his mouth and turned to the flipchart, there were no markers to be found anywhere! His lecture depended on six words—up/down, near/far, here/there. He decided to use the "invisible word" technique and asked his class to visualize these words on the flipchart as he "invisibly wrote" them. Throughout the next forty minutes as he referred and gestured to his flipchart with invisible words, his class knew precisely what he was saying!

One of Kevin's graduate students inadvertently tried the same thing a year later. Giving a talk about the twelve steps of Alcoholics Anonymous, this student began to list the twelve on the board. He wrote the numbers one through twelve with room for an explanation after each. The only problem was that after he filled in the first, he forgot to fill in the rest. Only numbers two through twelve were on the board with no explanation. After his well-presented lecture, he turned and said, "Oh my gosh, I forgot to write the rest of it!" Kevin took a chance. "Wait, let's see how well you did." Kevin stood up, pointed to a number and simply asked, "Which one is this?" The class not only knew which step was which—they also remembered the student's metaphor for each.

COACH'S COMMENTS

Question: At a big conference in my industry, the keynote speaker used a lot of digital photographs in her presentation and we loved it! Would this technique be good to use at work? Would I get laughed out of the boardroom?

Your coach says: Photos in PowerPoint presentations are a great idea. It personalizes and gathers interest. You can use them for serious reasons (to show geography, building sites, fashion trends, etc.) or you can use them with humor (coworkers after the holidays, the most recent company picnic). Most digital cameras come with easy instructions on saving the photos on your computer and they're easy to open and position in your talk. However, remember that just because you like it doesn't mean they will, or that it is appropriate for all audiences. Every audience is unique.

Consider teaching "invisibly." Cyndi often begins a session by asking each attendee to complete a sentence such as: "A great manager is like [an object in this room]." Then each person needs to explain why. After everybody contributes his or her object and reasoning, she points out each person one by one, and asks if the group can remember the person's object and reasoning. The group usually remembers 100 percent of the objects and reasons. The activity provides lessons in listening, how we remember through analogy and creativity, and it's done totally without visuals. It's learning invisibly.

Consider using the room itself. What is in the room, what is framed, what pictures, what kind of food, how about the service? Use what is available to you. When you get awesome service from the staff, comment on it and seek others' input. When the service is bad, ask how it could be improved. Consider using what is around you right now, right here. Take the chance. We've often seen pros use water pitchers and glasses to demonstrate attitude, goal setting, and other business-related concepts.

What is most important is that you "connect" with your visuals. This means you work with the visuals and not only as mere additions to your talk. They can become coteachers with you. Yes, your audience will remember you—but they may remember your visuals even more!

One way to "connect" is to ask the audience for their input as you use your visual. Never simply lecture, but ask. Never go on and on; stop and ask. Never ask and get one answer—ask again and listen. Use your audience as your final visual. They will have even better ideas than you do—and they tend to listen to one another even more than they will listen to you!

Take a chance and risk the benefits of a satisfied audience.

Part VI

Adapt to the Moment

37

When "Dr. Evil" Shows Up, Be Ready

- **Audience members who misbehave need your skilled approach and intervention.**
- **This is also an opportunity for persuasion and group interaction.**
- **Be careful not to let your fear dictate your response to what could be a delightful conflict.**

Some audience members want to talk, argue, and look better than the rest. Somehow these people will find you and your audience. And they will misbehave! Rather than try to fight them yourself, think about using peer pressure.

After Dr. Evil outlines his thoughts, move to the flipchart and summarize what he has said as accurately as you can in words or in a graphic image like three interlocking circles. Then ask: "What do you like most about this idea?" Take the responses as you normally would, then ask: "If you were to change this idea to make it closer to how you feel, what would you add?" This appears less threatening to Dr. Evil and allows for others to add to the learning.

Or, find the opposite of Dr. Evil's response and flipchart that as well. Put each flipchart at opposite ends of the classroom. Request that everyone stand up and physically locate themselves at one of the two poles or in between. Then facilitate a discussion with everyone standing where they have placed themselves and why they have done so. This lets you know (and more important, lets him know) how many are with him and how many are not.

These kinds of conflicts can truly be delightful if you will do just one thing—not take them personally. An obnoxious person is a person first. Let him have his "say," but not his "way." Kevin always approaches his worst audience member at the coffee break and says something like, "I am really glad you came today. You really spiced things up." They always laugh and then go on to explain their point more quietly—and Kevin has no more trouble with them. Their need for attention and power is answered when the presenter has paid attention and listened.

If your enemy is within you, work through your anxiety, nerves, and bad karma. Breathing is a vital function for presenters. You breathe differently when you get nervous—from the top of your chest instead of from deep within your chest. When you breathe differently, you also present differently—you look more confident, even if you don't always feel that way. Take a deep breath and remember you have something great for the audience, those who came to see and hear just you!

Form a community of learners. The burning questions and fun facts (chapter 25) help establish community among your participants, which is enormously helpful when you want to discuss and facilitate the program. Audiences composed of technical professionals are not always prepared for this. Don't be dismayed if they seem a little hesitant to join in. You might start with one of your colleagues to get the ball rolling. Peer pressure will take over and before you know it, a community will be formed.

Manage fear—yours and theirs. Be wary of how fear can outmatch the goal. When you deliver unpleasant news or when you face a hostile audience, make sure you prepare them for what you have to say. If you've done your homework ahead of time (phone interviews), then you can easily and effectively summarize their thinking on the topic and begin to introduce yours. You can also present "three possibilities of what I am going to say tonight. See if you can guess which one I believe to be true." When we label fear as fear, it controls us. When we label fear as excitement, we stay in control. Which would you prefer?

Watch out for guest experts gone amuck. When you bring

others in to present for or with you, always consider yourself the copresenter. Rehearse them ahead of time. Have a signal or clue between you that allows you to speak. Tune them in to the underlying politics and purpose of the meeting.

COACH'S COMMENTS

Your coach says: Whatever you do, avoid your first impulse. Anything you do will be better than that. Your first impulse tends to be either anger or defensiveness. It's not good to be angry or defensive in front of a crowd; they quickly begin to mistrust you.

Use self-disclosure strategically. Don't tell the audience what you think about an issue they are debating until you are ready to shut down the discussion. The longer you wait to contribute, the more they will discuss. Avoid letting the "we" become "them versus me." Sometimes it is easy, despite your best intentions, to come across as a know-it-all. For years, Cyndi has had a funny button on her bulletin board that says, "People who think they know it all really annoy those of us who do." We often know more than the audience does, but thinking this way will get you into trouble when you are the presenter. Consider viewing yourself less as an expert (even if you are one) and more as a teacher.

Always have an air of inquiry, interest in the other person, a question that seeks more, and a kind of child's innocence. When you take this approach, it is more likely the audience will feel you are one of them, rather than you being a big shot.

**Humility goes a long way for presenters,
especially the expert ones.**

When Your Presenter Doesn't Show, You Can Still Shine

- **Sometimes presenters don't show up.**
- **The audience does.**
- **You need to do something.**

It will happen to you. Yes, with the best laid plans your audience will show and your presenter will not. And, of course, everyone will be looking at you expectantly.

Here is your chance to do very well, even if you don't know the material. Your boss will be impressed. The audience will greet you afterward like a celebrity. And you will even enjoy the experience! Here's the secret: Let the audience talk!

This is what the pros do when they have no idea what to do. They hand over the microphone.

Kevin once attended a professional meeting where the third of three presenters on a technical topic was stuck at the airport and unable to present as planned. Her substitute did what too many people do in his situation: he said he "didn't know much about the topic" but "was going to give it a shot." He then pretended to know the material, read every slide word for word, and tried to be funny with each slide—all thirty-seven of them. This was late in the afternoon and he was the only thing between the audience and the bar. It was an understandable and crucial error.

Here is what you can do if and when it happens to you. There are many short steps and they're all important and deserve clear instructions from you to get attention.

First, announce that the next speaker has been delayed and then say, "This will give all of us a rare opportunity. I will need your help and when our presenter does show, we'll be ready for her." Then immediately say, "Everyone please stand up, look around, find two partners, and get into small groups of three with anyone you want except the person sitting next to you. Just for fun, let's do it in complete silence. When you have your partners, just sit down away from any tables."

Remember that every part of what you are telling them is important; don't leave out a bit of it. We will tell you why later.

Now, ask each small group to take four minutes to introduce themselves and to tell one another what they most wanted to learn from this session. Give them time to do this. Then ask for some to share: "What did you notice you had in common?" Listen to a few, react, expand, mostly listen, perhaps repeat or paraphrase what they are saying.

Now tell them as a group that they have twenty-five minutes to do the following: "Please look over the presenter's PowerPoint notes, discuss what you notice that is old news to you, new news to you, intriguing or perplexing news to you. Your task at the end of this twenty-five minutes is to tell the rest of us the three most significant things your group learned about this presentation. We will give you poster paper and markers and we want you to, in a few very large words or, better, in a symbol, to tell us what your group learned."

Ask for questions or clarifications and then let them loose. Afterward, you can have them report to the large group. This is a conventional, time-tested strategy and it will always work.

A more creative choice is to call time and have them stay in their groups, combine with another group to form a group of six, and to teach the other group what their group learned. Their task for the next nine minutes is to talk, teach, and ultimately notice what they have in common with one another.

Then ask the group to hang both of their poster papers on the wall next to each other and to share only one word that best summarizes their group's conclusion and to write that word at the top of the papers.

Now have half of the group stay with their posters and ask the other groups to go group to group for two minutes each to hear their report. Groups of six report to another group of six.

If your presenter never shows up, all the better. If your presenter shows up, ask him or her to wait, to edit their talk, and finally to move around the groups as a special guest.

This is one guaranteed career builder. It may even make you a professional speaker—or, rather, facilitator.

COACH COMMENTS

Your coach says: All of these steps are important because they get the audience into an "adult learning mode" and get them past the disappointment over not having a presenter. No matter how sophisticated the audience, give your instructions in simple fourth-grade language ("look around, find two partners," etc.). This action immediately gets them from a "listening mode" into an "activity mode." This is also why it is important not to interrupt the activity if and when your presenter does show up. If you do interrupt them, they will not be listening anyway. Let them complete the activity, give the presenter something to do ("visit each group and ask what they are learning"), and be confident that you are in charge.

39

Don't Let Murphy's Law Surprise You

- **Bad things happen to good presenters.**
- **Treat all hotel staff with respect and admiration.**
- **The environment of your presentation is as important as your presentation.**
- **You need to be sensitive to the room temperature as well as your content.**

Like everything in life, avoiding meeting mayhem; achieving meeting magic starts with the little things—room lighting and audiovisual needs—as well as larger issues like how best to foster team dynamics and work toward real solutions to pressing organizational problems. Logistics can encourage your participants to feel comfortable and ready to contribute *or* leave them tearing their hair out and fleeing to the hallway for "important" cell phone calls that take up the rest of the morning.

Keep them in their seats focused on you by eliminating distractions. Be the first one in, and the last one out. You should be the first person in the room to doublecheck, to get the feel of the room, and to greet the first attendees. Small audiovisual considerations will make a big difference in your confidence level for starting the day. Yes, the audiovisual pros will be there for you, but in reality, they are often less concerned about the total picture than you are. Make them work to help you look good. When you are confident, you will look, sound, act, and be more persuasive.

Assume nothing but change. Check on the room the night before and the day of your session. Even if you arrive an hour before the attendees, don't be surprised if things have been altered. Hotel staffs have a way of changing things in the middle of the night. Ask the hotel representative to help you. Consider sending two versions of room setup instructions—one English and one Spanish. Use more than words; include a diagram or pictures. The setup people are in a hurry and will respond to less rather than more in terms of text. Draw what you want and you will be more likely to get it.

Corporate maintenance staffs can also surprise you by moving things around to a pattern they know. If the room is not to your liking, have it changed immediately. You may need to start moving chairs yourself. Only you know what you want and what the attendees need.

If you are in a room for several hours or all day, you and your audience will need the energy that only light can bring. Turn the room lighting as bright as possible while still being able to see the screen for visuals. In hotels and conference centers, the house audiovisual people have been trained to set lights dimly for the computer visuals screen. Boost everyone's spirits with more light, especially after 2:30 P.M., when most audiences tend to lose energy. This is important. Keep the lights up even if they fade your screen a bit. You are more important than your visuals and you and the audience need to see one another clearly.

Be high-maintenance with your audiovisual provider. During preplanning, request that your audiovisual provider arrive at least one hour before starting time. This is not an unusual request, and it is essential for you to test the microphones ahead of time. Know the audiovisual person's name, brief him or her on what the meeting is for, what you want from them, and ask their advice (except about lighting). Check with them at breaks to ask how you sounded. Also, ask a colleague or attendee who will tell you the truth.

It is no small feat to prepare the environment for a meeting.

Remember that meeting you attended where the room was too hot, too cold, you couldn't hear clearly, you forgot that other participants' name, and the food was marginal? If you can remember those meetings clearly, so can those who attend your next meeting.

Great meetings do not just happen. You design them.

FROM THE PROS

"When you know you're going to be miked with a lavaliere, plan ahead of time where you will clip the mike on your clothing; this is especially important for women. Women should also be aware of the lavaliere wire and put the wire through clothing ahead of time and put the receiver in a pocket. Be aware that hair or clothes touching the mike will rustle. Also, be aware that the room may have hot spots, and if you move close to a speaker you may get feedback. Walk around the stage with the mike on to get a feel for any interference or hot spots. If speakers are in the ceiling, avoid walking below them.

I videotape a lot of speakers. One mistake a lot of people make is that they freeze up and don't act natural when they're being videotaped. Also, as soon as they're finished they look away or leave; if they'd look right at the camera and smile, it would give a more final touch. The best speakers also work well with camera placement and movement. They don't move really fast and they move with purpose, especially when being taped.

"What do the best presenters do? In my opinion, the best presenters are really prepared and relaxed in the first thirty seconds or one minute. If they're really prepared and relaxed in that time, it sets the mood.

—Steve, video producer with twelve years of experience

COACH'S COMMENTS

Question: How do I look cool, calm, and collected during an emergency situation?

Your coach says: Don't panic. Assign out loud the person you have preassigned to be your buddy to go and check on things and then make a decision to continue, take a break, or seek shelter in an emergency. Remember, the audience doesn't know what to do, either, so they will look to you to decide. One speaker said during a blackout, "Now, if you will, visualize . . ." The crowd roared and he finished his speech.

40

When Asked to Edit, Be Prepared

- **A pro is ready to edit on the spot.**
- **The reason they can edit is because they have prepared to do so.**
- **Shorter is more difficult, yet more satisfying than longer.**

For any presentation, be prepared to edit on the spot. Think about it. When is the last time you went to a meeting that ran on time? There are so many variables. An introducer's words may take five minutes instead of two. A lunch may be served more slowly than anticipated. The dessert course often takes forever. The speaker before you can inspire a long, intense question/answer period, leaving you with ten minutes. In light of all these possibilities, the pros are ready to shorten their talks at a moment's notice.

Rise to the challenge! If you plan ahead, you can respond just like the pros the next time you hear, "Could you shorten it a bit?" You can become so ready to adapt that you almost look forward to it! Improvisation artists do. The art of improvisation is the art of thinking smart on your feet, or at least to appear to. It's important to show no stress or anger—instead, carry on with confidence. In fact, a sense of humor and a smile at this point will carry you even further in the audience's eyes

There are six steps to the editing success. First, look at your key points and know which two or three you could cut on short notice. For example, if you're reporting employee responses to a satisfaction survey, select six, but be ready to pick only four if you need to. Highlight those four so you can find them easily.

Second, be ready to remove any background information that could be sent via e-mail or as handouts after you speak. Then, when you do take it out, don't apologize for lack of time, merely say, "I'll send you more details via e-mail later today."

Third, as you speak, pick up your pace without rushing. Get right to the point, cite your best examples, and keep the pace moving. Everyone in the audience will appreciate the fact that you honor their schedules. Make sure you are not rushing or speaking faster—simply pick up the pace, get right to the content and the examples, and move on.

Fourth, have a symbol ready that represents everything at once in a visual way. For example, three circles or triangles can represent three things and can serve to unify an entire concept. Or create one slide that represents your main concept and use it instead of six detailed slides.

Fifth, know your PowerPoint well enough that you can skip to certain sections, eliminating others without the audience knowing. Imagine you had planned to use five quotes but now want to skip the first four and go immediately to the fifth. To do this, hit the laptop keyboard number of the slide that has the quote you want to move to, and it will take you to where you want to be.

Finally, check Chapter 68 of this book for details on having a second presentation ready. Have on hand your "just in case" version (your second presentation) and make sure that version is shorter by at least a third.

COACH'S COMMENTS

Your coach says: Pilots always know where the nearest airport is, just in case. When there is trouble, the pilot has a ready alternative. So do wise presenters. Know what you'll emphasize in case you are asked to cut your speech short. Know what you'll include if asked to go a little longer. Consider what question you'll use when you have time for some audience interaction. When you are ready, like the pilot, you will always have an alternative. And your landing will always be smooth!

Simplicity impacts your audience. Your shorter presentation will probably be better than your original. When you have an eye on editing, you eliminate wordy descriptions and repetitions. You will be clearer and have more impact, and that's more challenging. In seventeenth-century France, writer Blaise Pascal wrote: "I have made this letter longer, because I have not had the time to make it shorter."

Force yourself to take the red pencil (or your word processor's editing tool) to your talk. When you're asked to edit on the spot, you'll be glad you did the pre-work. If you've ever tried to write a short bio or program blurb of fifty words or less, you know how hard this can be. Fifty words is a common maximum in publishing programs and reports possibly because it's so hard to write that few words to describe something. There must be a lesson there.

When you put pen to paper, be conscious of every thought and the words will come—just remember that written words are very different when spoken out loud. Practice out loud.

41

When Asked for Your Opinion, Listen First

- **Beware of too much self-disclosure.**
- **Seek out the diverse opinions of your audience.**
- **Wait to reveal your own opinion, if at all.**

As you present, be prepared for the time when your audience may want your opinion. When you are seen as an "expert," audiences frequently want to know where you stand on an issue. It is not always helpful to tell them.

It's better to wait. First, to give your own perspective takes them off the hook for expressing their own opinion and their own learning. It is much more difficult to come to your own decision, but it is ultimately more useful. People often avoid stating their real feelings, especially in a work environment.

Second, it sets you up to be disagreed with. If the audience doesn't like what you say, they may decide the rest of what you are saying isn't worth much, either. Consider the last time someone you respected let you know who they voted for (not your candidate!) in the most recent presidential election. "How could someone so smart be so stupid?" you're thinking. Audience's thoughts can quickly take the same route.

Third, if you tell the audience your conclusions too quickly or give your opinion at all, you can shortcut the real fun and suspense of your talk. When is a birthday more fun for you—before the gifts are unwrapped or after?

COACH'S COMMENTS

Your coach says: Always be prepared and have an alternative ready. When you are given more time, remember you don't have to use it all. Audiences always appreciate getting out a few minutes early. Sometimes an example or two—a rehearsed example or two—will take ten to fifteen minutes. If you add audience Q&A, that is another ten to fifteen minutes. Just because you have been given extra time does not mean you must talk the entire time. Facilitate! (For more on that, flip to chapter 51.)

Try using the following techniques to stimulate original thoughts within your audience, rather than revealing your opinion and being open for judgment.

- **Use a question.** "What do you think?" is a great way to "ask back"—a time-tested technique first invented by psychiatrists. Or use the unexpected, "Gee, I don't know. What a great question! What do you think?" This is especially useful if you are a very knowledgeable expert. Your audience will be surprised and complimented.

- **Use your hands.** Economists use this technique often: "On the one hand . . . and on the other hand . . ." President Harry Truman once requested that he be sent a "one-handed economist" so that he could get a final answer! This is a great way to help audiences understand the issues that might need to be taken into consideration. When you use this technique, consider actually using your hands as gestures. It helps the audience "see" the difference.

- **Use history.** Knowing how others have approached the same problem can be very useful indeed. "When we talked with past presidents who faced this challenge, we found that . . ." is a very credible way to begin a response. Or how about, "For the last five years, that has been a popular question in this area." History may not always repeat itself, but like personal experience, it is hard to argue with it!

- **Use an analogy.** "This reminds me of the famous story about a goat, a pig, and a salesman . . ." or "This is like shooting an arrow without a target. What is our goal for this discussion?"

- **Use a metaphor.** "Dams are designed to hold water and to let water go—the question is how much is enough, how much is too much?"

- **Use a teaching technique.** "Rather than tell you what I think right now, let me tell you instead what I see are the facts and the limits of the problem at hand." Then go to the flipchart and draw a box. Put some issues inside the box, some outside, and speak to the forces that are "acting on our community," etc.

- **Use the group.** "May I ask you all to indulge me for a moment? Please break up into groups of three and take five minutes to decide together what you think my opinion will be based on what you have heard tonight and what you know of me." Let them talk. None of the groups will agree! When they make their reports, chart them on the flipchart. Then end with, "I am really embarrassed! Your ideas were much, much better than mine! I am going to reconsider!"

As important as it is to you, your opinion is mostly impressive only to you—consider keeping it to yourself.

FROM THE RANKS

"When I was first promoted to project manager, I was asked to give a half-hour presentation on a new idea to the marketing team. I worked hard and came up with a new form. I planned my entire presentation around this form. The day arrived, and after the guy before me, the question of new forms came up. The VP of marketing yelled, 'Not another new form! Anything but that! We have too many new forms.' I began sweating bullets; luckily there was a break.

"I considered not showing up after the break. I could say I was ill. But then my mind reverted me to seventh grade—to being a running back on the football team. I only had to remember two calls from the quarterback: 'Pitch left' and 'Pitch right.' Now, ordinarily this would be simple, but during an important game, I purposefully did not wear my massive hearing aids under the helmet (I've been severely hearing-impaired my whole life) and just guessed at what the quarterback was saying. Needless to say, I did not do well that game. When the coach called me in later, I was afraid I was getting kicked off the team. Instead, he said, 'Well, Costello, I'd like you to be our quarterback; since you can't hear the plays, you have to call them.'

"This was the story I told after the break. Somehow I tied it into working with what you have to make the best of new ideas and what a great manager my coach was. I really learned to listen to the presentations ahead of mine that day. I still do."

—Rich, an instructional technology professional

42

Beware of the Two-Year-Old in You

- **A two-year-old is self-focused.**
- **A two-year-old blames others.**
- **A two-year-old lacks patience.**

Presenters often have a great deal of fun. What's not to like? You are presenting your best material, the audience usually likes you, and you are in the spotlight. Be careful not to let this go to your head. Stay emotionally mature.

It's not about you. Professionals are often advised to be careful not to believe their own advertising. Ego is a very big danger here. Guard against it at all costs. Generally audiences like you and will permit you to have fun as long as you are having fun along with them, not in front of them and certainly not without them.

This is why the best speakers, entertainers, humorists, comedians, and actors all learn to control how much fun they are having in relationship to how much fun the audience is having. They focus on their task, not on themselves. We have said it before in this book (and we will say it again!) that to be a great speaker is to be audience-focused. This is not an easy task. It is too easy to be driven by what you want and what you think is fun and funny. Any comedian will tell you—only the audience knows for sure!

Don't blame the audience. Professional comedians test new material every time they go onstage. They never rely on all new material. They test it to see if the audience agrees with them as to its humor. Kevin used to tell a short story, actually a throwaway line, in every one of his first three hundred speeches. He thought it was funny. It never got a laugh. But he persisted. Maybe it was his timing, he thought, maybe the audience, maybe the phase of the moon. One day he thought, rightfully so, this is only funny to me! He now only tells this story to himself—with a painful smile.

COACH'S COMMENTS

Your coach says: Some truths may offend. Be aware of yourself, especially your annoying self. Are you a compulsive "pen clicker"? Do you snort to clear your nose? Do others comment on your laugh . . . and maybe not in a complimentary way? Do you blow your nose and then shake hands with the person who was your witness? One famous, very famous speaker is a constant "lip licker" as he speaks. This is most likely something he is unaware of and it probably doesn't limit his ability to sell books, but it is difficult to watch.

Do you have a tendency to tell off-color jokes? Do you use demeaning language such as "little lady" or "darlin' " or tell blonde jokes? Watch your use of vocabulary such as "awesome," "guys," "so cool," "ya know," "totally," "rad," etc. You will rarely hear your boss or your boss's boss speak that way. If they do, think about how you feel when you hear it. Stay aware of your mannerisms and habits. Think to yourself that you are "on" all the time . . . because you are.

Similarly, Cyndi finally gave up using a list of ten management tips that she really liked and honed it down to six. It took her a while to realize that ten were too many. Her clue came when eyes began to glaze over and people rarely mentioned the tips afterward. This was not the audience's problem; it was the presenter's. Audiences usually give candid feedback if the presenter will learn to acknowledge it.

Don't jump to conclusions. A two-year-old is a master at the impatient approach: "I want a cookie *now*! I want her toy *now*! I don't want to *share*!" That impatience still resides within most people, long beyond the age of two. When presenting, you may find that your talk is not going exactly as you planned. There may be more questions than you anticipated or lots of interruptions or a disagreeable manager who seems to take issue with all your points. Be patient.

Try to remember that most difficulties work out in time. Assumptions are not wise choices. Medieval English philosopher William of Occam wrote, "When learning about life and people, make no more assumptions than are absolutely necessary. Ask and observe." This is true for the emotionally mature presenter as well.

Focus on your task, not on yourself.

43

Inquire, Observe, and Learn

- **You are "it."**
- **Meet and prepare your audience.**
- **Use coffee breaks strategically.**

No meeting is casual or unimportant. Some meetings may be urgent, some critical. Some may be business reviews. With each meeting, you are onstage. Your business profile is out in front of everyone.

We have sat through many meetings that happen "after the meeting." These meetings are with the leaders reflecting on what happened and who made it happen. Names are used, body language noticed, tone of voice remarked upon, and deliverables reviewed. In nearly every case, the person being talked about had no idea what was said. He or she may not find out until their next performance appraisal!

COACH'S COMMENTS

Your coach says: Become curious about everything. Let no one and nothing escape your inescapable curiosity. Be childlike in your interest and encouraging in your questioning of others. Here's a standard question you can ask of executives and taxi drivers, busboys and physicians, dropouts and Ph.D.s. It is simply, "What is the most challenging thing about what you do?" You will always receive an answer rich with detail, emotion, and new information. These stories can often find their way into your talks and responses to Q&As.

Treat every meeting like it is the first impression your boss or your boss's boss will form of you. Leave them talking about your most impressive qualities with some simple business strategies. The presenter who can simplify without losing the importance of the meaning is of real value in today's business climate.

Treat every meeting with an attitude of great importance. Consider who called the meeting and do what you can attitudinally to support their cause. If you disagree with the meeting, then at least support the meeting as an opportunity to discuss differences and commonalities.

Prepare for who will be there. Do you know them personally? Is their picture on the corporate Web site? Any chance you can meet them by phone or in person prior to the actual meeting? Then write on a small note card those things you want to accomplish at this meeting. Also write out a few open-ended questions so if the meeting gets offtrack or emotional, you will have a visual reminder of what you want from the meeting.

Plan your contribution through collaboration. Don't be afraid to talk to others in advance about what they want from the meeting. This affords you a great opportunity to speak to your needs as well . . . collaboratively. Encourage, affirm, and animate the meeting attendees. Actively participate. Utilize positive body language. Care for your contributions no matter how minor they might appear. Frequently summarize what the group is saying.

Follow up and deliver. Are you supposed to get a report out in two weeks? Do so in thirteen days . . . or in one week! When you notice someone has been hurt or is feeling down as a result of the meeting, have lunch with them. Be known for being sensitive, for following up, and for focusing on what is going right.

Prepare for every meeting with intentional design. Coffee breaks are an excellent opportunity to meet your boss's boss, the CEO, or better yet, the CEO's administrative coordinator. Also, consider it an opportunity to meet with your worst enemy in the organization. There's no complicated strategy involved. Simply meet and make small talk. Follow their lead. Be personable. Don't focus on a project or anything else that has an agenda. Pursue your hidden agenda: to get in the world and the environment of the other.

More often than not, professionals stay away from their boss's boss or the CEO. They are quietly polite in elevators. They rely on the superior to greet them. If this isn't career suicide, it is at least career malnourishment. Take a moment to be interested in who they are and briefly let them know who you are. Never assume they will remember you from the last time, and always introduce yourself with a connecting point:

- "Mr. Defano, I'm Maria Esperanza, from marketing. I'm the lucky person who spilled coffee on you last year at this very conference! Remember me!?"

- "Dr. Johnson, I'm Howard Emerson from accounting, and I'm a weekend sailor like you."

- "Steve, I'm John English, one of your company's customers, and I just want to tell you how pleased I am with your sales-people, especially Bob Thompson."

All of these quick, to-the-point introductions will make the other person feel at ease, identify you in a unique way, and initiate a conversation, however brief.

You will only be known if you utilize your informal opportunities with the people in power. When you can, seat yourself next to the person you want to talk to or influence. Initiate the conversation. Get in their world. Seize the moment before someone else does.

Coffee breaks are not for relaxing.

THREE WAYS TO CONNECT

- Watch those who look interested, are smiling, nodding, and show energy. There is no better way to connect than to work with the connection you already have.

- When some seem marginally interested, move physically closer to them. They will pay more attention and will "like" you and your message more because of it. Presence helps build trust.

- With those who are actively resistant, look bored, are e-mailing, try two things simultaneously: ignore them mentally and move closer to them physically. Physical closeness will increase their attention span. Ignoring them mentally will keep you sane!

44

It's the Norm, Not the Exception

- **Understanding the difference between what is normal and what is exceptional will make you exceptional.**

- **You can be in charge of what happens and what might happen.**

- **You can be and think like other presenters, just don't act like them!**

It is normal to be apprehensive before you go on. Use your nervous energy to be better. Remind yourself of the people in the audience we often forget about. Someone out there is experiencing very difficult circumstances. Someone else is hopeless. Someone else is on the verge of being fired. Still another needs you to be your best—not your perfect best, but your best at making a positive difference in that moment.

It is normal to feel as though you could have prepared a little more. Given more time, we all would. However, now is now. You are on. No more prep time. And, in fact, more prep time is not always what we really need—thinking time is what we may need. When you are in front of an audience and you are doing well, you really will have a conversation with the audience and more will come from you than you might imagine.

It is normal to want the audience's approval. You won't do a very good job, though, if you focus only on that. Instead, focus on what you know and what you know they need to hear and understand. This will provide the fuel to say what they need to hear—and the courage!

It is normal to want more time, more technology, more help, more respect (!), more, more, more. You have what you have. It is normal to make a mistake. Very "normle"! Don't let it sidetrack you. They came to hear you, not your perfection.

COACH'S COMMENTS

Your coach says: Develop a routine for yourself on how you give a speech. Perhaps you have an introduction, then three points, then a closing summary. Or you might open with a story that unifies the presentation and move into your bullet points and end with a summary slide. Always have some very general outline in your head or on a note card, so that if you get into trouble you will know where you are at all times. When this is the norm, it is easier to remember.

Many presenters demand; make sure you never do. Many presenters want what they want, but your job is to give the audience what it wants and needs. Many presenters think they are special—others know that the audience is what's special.

It is the exceptional speaker who can know and experience all of this and still be available for the audience.

Part VII

Propel the Image

45

Look Like You Mean It

- **When your audience looks at you, what and whom do they see?**

- **Invest in your appearance to make an impact.**

- **Looks matter, like it or not.**

Be very aware of how you dress for your presentation. How do you look, really? Many people will use your appearance to fortify their impressions of you, both good and bad. You can make a positive impression with a different hairstyle and newer, dressier clothes. You may be used to you, but others are very aware that your style may be passé. We often suggest that presenters work with an image coach—someone who is honest and skilled with the messages sent by visual detail; for example, how hairstyle and tie color affect credibility. One person who took this advice called us thirty days later and said: "Some are wondering what's different. Some even suspect I am interviewing for another job!"

Be especially aware if it's your first time before a group. First impressions are subjective. It's difficult for your audience to be totally unbiased when meeting you for the first time. They make judgments and assumptions so they can put you in a box—a box that allows them to operate. This is the way the mind works in person perception. It judges quickly and ruthlessly and you're rarely given much of a second chance to change it. This seems fairly intimidating, but if you plan ahead in some simple ways, you can make the impression you want—or at least come very close!

Invest in how you look. Buy a "business wardrobe." Find an unbiased hairstylist and ask for a new hairdo. Go for a makeup consultation. Speak more clearly (and loudly). Look others in the eye. Stand up straight. Gesture for emphasis. Wear shoes you feel great in and make sure they're polished. A pro we know has his shoes polished at the airport or in the hotel immediately before he presents. The confidence you feel knowing you look your best communicates credibility. Audiences believe confident speakers much more quickly than they believe those who appear reticent.

At a Catholic Bishops' installation, many representatives went up to the altar one by one to greet the new bishop in a show of welcome and solidarity. Most were dressed for the occasion. One had on a sweatshirt with the inscription of a school on it. As he walked down the stairs to the congregation, many smiled or snickered at how incongruous he looked at such a formal ceremony. Had he looked in the mirror? Maybe. Had he asked someone he trusted, "How do I look to greet the bishop today in front of ten thousand onlookers?" The answer to that question might have prompted a wardrobe change.

Professional speakers are extremely particular about how they look in front of a group. Women invest in bright, energetically colored suit jackets and skirts or pants that flatter—never reveal. Trends change from year to year, but a neckline accent of some type is important to draw the audience's eyes toward your face. We coach female speakers to wear a bright brooch or flower on their lapel and for men to wear a tie that brings out their eye color. As a presenter, your main tool is your face—your eyes, smile, and facial expressions. Make sure your face gets accented! White and pale shirts are good for this reason as well.

Look like the job you want or the executive you want to remember you. Always dress a notch above what the audience might expect. Always, always bring a jacket and wear it to begin your talk. You can then remove it for any reason—temperature in the room, casual mood of the crowd, or to reinforce a "let's get down to work" tone in the presentation. Some pros have a planned spot when they take off jackets, hats, or ties to make a point.

COACH'S COMMENTS

Your coach says: Forgive me, as your coach, for sounding a bit cynical: People judge you by how you look. Before you open your mouth, before you get a chance to remind yourself that you are "on," before you can even get to know them . . . how you look affects how they will listen to you. Be purposeful in your dress, your hair, your mannerisms, and your look. Even if you don't feel confident, act like you are. Don't look in a mirror and check how you think you look, rather check how others will probably look at you. Find an adviser for your hair and clothes and periodically check in with them. Tell them who your audience is and see what they say.

Take seriously how you appear. Show you are aware and alert at meetings when you're not up front. Smile. Keep your arms and hands on the table rather than in your lap. Sit upright. Use a pen and take notes—not all the time, but often. It's important people see your eyes, not just the top of your head. Plan your contributions in advance of the meetings. Affirm others when they contribute. Listen to other presenters with the same dedication that you would like others to listen to you. Summarize the contents of the meetings you attend periodically in front of the group. This is great practice in both speaking and listening.

Research how you might impact and influence. Call attendees prior to your meetings and preinterview them about their goals. Welcome attendees with a firm handshake. Ask interesting questions and follow-up questions. When asked for your business card, have it handy in a nice cardholder or easy-to-reach pocket. Don't be caught digging through your purse or briefcase. Ask others for their cards and handle them with care and interest. We can learn a lot from Asian cultures, particularly Japanese, with respect to elegant business card handling. Be focused on others, not on yourself. Send thank-you notes.

If you do these things, you will not be invisible anymore. Like it or not, people judge a book by its cover. When they see the same old you day after day, they expect very little that is different. They literally don't even see you. When they hear you contribute in the same way at each and every meeting, they literally don't hear you. When they look at you, whom do they see?

**Make yourself over, inside and out,
and experiment with a new look.**

THREE QUICK IMAGE IMPROVEMENTS

- **Polish your shoes or have them polished at the hotel or airport.** For men, this is almost always seen as a sign of a professional—it is one of the first things executives notice when they are checking you out.

- **Take an invigorating shower with a partner before you speak, to keep the color in your skin.** No partner? No mind! Refresh yourself in the hotel's pool, or even just by putting on a fresh shirt. The airline clubs often have showers, and it may well be worth the time to appear your very best.

- **Lightly spray or gel your hair so it's the least of your worries.** One last trip to the mirror is a good idea along with a "how do I look?" to a bellman, friend, or friend-to-be in your audience just before you go on. Performers have professional assistants who do this for them behind the curtain just before they walk out—you can, too!

46

Sound Like You Mean It

- **Metaphors mean special things to audiences.**
- **Every audience likes a meaningful "in the moment" experience.**
- **Four easy techniques help you sound like you mean it.**

Harness the power of metaphors. Sometimes we hear an audience member use a metaphor that simply captures everything we are saying: "So this project is a little like mountain climbing—not for the faint of heart!" they might say. Use the mountain climbing then in your answer. "Indeed, this is like a mountain climbing expedition in three ways: It is risky, as you say; it is also very possible with the right team and the right resources; and, most of all, with the right training we can climb the mountain. It is before us—waiting." This kind of an answer effectively powers through the message. It also compliments the contributor.

Metaphors are often more helpful than facts. You can be even more powerful when you combine the metaphor *with* the facts. What if you had a mountain climber in your audience (which you learned from the fun facts warm-up at the beginning). You could say, "Bob, you climb mountains. What is the greatest challenge in climbing a real mountain?" When he answers, regardless of what he says, then ask the group, "How is that like the challenge before us?" You'll have them all thinking creatively.

Another way to "sound like you mean it" is to frame your message constantly in terms of participant concerns, even when you need to be focused on a specific topic. Remember to work from burning questions and keep that chart in the forefront of your work with your audience. The more you speak to and of their concerns, the more you will gather from them. You will revitalize the group's energy level whenever you make your message group-centered. You might say, "Sandra, your earlier mention of the new wave of competitors seems to be popping up a lot today. Clearly, this is on everyone's mind." Or, "John, I'm glad you got the pricing issue on the table right away. It's come up several times this morning." People love to hear their ideas and their names mentioned positively again and again.

COACH'S COMMENTS

Your coach says: Forgive me again, as your coach, for sounding a bit cynical: People judge you by how you sound. When you do open your mouth, do so purposefully. Watch your volume, the way you laugh, the pace of your questions, and the speed of your speaking. Some of us have a natural tendency to trail off the last bit of our sentences and therefore they have less volume and less impact. Some people make even declarative sentences a question. Be on guard here. Tape yourself and listen for a while to what others hear from you.

A third strategy is to be prepared, in charge, and ready. Smile, work with confidence, and don't look at your watch—ever! (Use a large face clock or a timer on a table in front of you.) Participants have mentioned speakers looking at their watches as negative points on evaluations. Details do stand out when you're up in front! Speak with volume and authority, move around the room, ask the audience to paraphrase others' contributions, raise open-ended questions, and never rush your presentation (when in doubt, cut material and make sure you speak to your summary slides).

Finally, use one of the best and simplest ways to "sound like you mean it"—show your summary slide first. This "last slide first" propels you and the audience into the content quickly, avoids a last-minute rush, and says you mean business. Few things are worse than a meandering opening where the speaker is trying to find his or her balance, and the audience is looking for the exit!

Your audience wants an experience, and they want you to be in charge of your own voice. Sound like you mean it.

47

Don't Fall into the Apology Trap

- **Don't begin with an apology.**
- **Don't include apologies at any point unless the roof falls in.**
- **Don't end with an apology.**

Too many presenters begin and end with apologies, also sprinkling them throughout their talks. We have heard apologies from presenters at all levels in the organization, all professions, all types of volunteers, and at all types of social events. Here are some of the common apologies that may sound familiar to you, too:

- **"I won't take long. I know you're all ready for lunch."**
- **"I know you've heard this material before. But I need to review it anyway."**
- **"For those of you who are technologically challenged, I apologize for . . ."**
- **"You don't know me, but I . . ."**
- **"I know we're over time, and I'll try to do my best to get you out of here as soon as possible."**
- **"Well, I don't have much time, and I have a lot to say so I guess I'd better get started."**

- "Maybe this has already come up earlier today, and I'm sorry if it has . . ."
- "You probably can't read this slide, but it says . . ."
- "If I had my slides with me I could show you . . ."
- "I'll try to make up time; I know we're behind in the agenda."
- "If the lighting were better in here, you'd see that . . ."
- "I'm not a great speaker, but here goes."
- "I know it's been a long day for you and I'll be brief."
- "I'm sorry you don't all have a copy of this data."
- "This slide is wrong; I apologize."
- "If I had the current data, I could show you . . ."
- "This is an old study, but I thought I'd use it to . . ."
- "Well, I'm sure you're glad that's it . . . unless there are any questions."
- "I see my time is up, and I apologize for all the slides."
- "I hope this has been useful. Good night."

Do you know what the audience feels and thinks when you say these things? Nothing! They don't care. All they know is they're still in the room or on the conference call with you and they have to listen to you anyway, unless their cell phone rings with a dire emergency. The most they may feel is annoyance—annoyance that you're alerting them to something basically unimportant to them. It's your problem, not theirs, they're thinking.

Presenters fall into the apology trap too often. Rarely is it necessary to apologize for time, material, audiovisuals, or agenda changes. Unless the problem is blatant—heat and lights going off, a tornado or hurricane, or missing essential handouts—you can still have a successful talk, express your point, and even earn your audience's liking and respect in spite of it all.

Keep apology out of your opening. We have written many pages about your opening in this book. An opening is very important and should never, ever be an apology. Even if something happens right before you speak, ignore it and proceed as planned with your inspirational opening.

Keep apology out of your talk. Most of the time, you have a captive audience; they have to listen to you as part of their jobs, their social etiquette, or responsibility, or their commitment to a cause. They want to listen to an interesting, credible, dynamic speaker who has something worthwhile to say, not someone wrapped up in apology. We have heard speakers apologize for their team, their research, their mistakes, their data, their presentation, their schedule, their lack of organization, and their wardrobe. Who cares?

COACH'S COMMENTS

Your coach says: "We'll have to move quickly through the rest of this material" is nothing more than a speaker who has planned poorly. "I'm sorry we don't have time to cover all of this in detail" is a pathetic way to work with an audience—again, poor planning. "I'm not really sure what you mean by ABC but XYZ" is a poor excuse for an unconcerned speaker. Don't apologize; just say what you are going to do. Instead of "moving quickly" you can say, "there are three critical points here." Instead of the time apology, tell them you have just enough time to cover ABC.

Keep apology out of your conclusion. When you end your talk, be proud and confident outwardly, even if you are quaking inside. If you're moving into a Q&A session, do it positively:

"I look forward now to any questions you may have." If there are none, either say "thank you" or come up with one on your own. Never apologize for the late hour or the lack of questions. It makes you look less confident.

Dynamic speakers never say they're sorry.

48

Become One with Your Microphone

- **Always use a microphone.**
- **Wear it high and in the middle.**
- **Use the full potential of the microphone for greatest impact.**

One famous professional speaker, a well-known author and lecturer, always asks his audiovisual people to increase the volume of his microphone just before he begins. He bellows into the microphone and is known for his . . . volume! He uses the microphone to accomplish his goal—he wants the audience to pay attention.

You don't have to bellow, but you do need to be in control of the technology. Doing so means wearing a mike; wear it high and in the middle on your tie or blouse, and test it for volume, feedback, and clarity throughout the room. Yes, arrive early to do so.

The reason you use a microphone in almost every situation is so every person in the room including those with a hearing loss who don't know they have a hearing loss can hear you. There are plenty of these people in your world and you only need a few in your audience to cause you to lose your impact. Don't be one of those presenters who says: "Oh, I don't need the mike. I've got a loud voice." We think they say that because they are secretly afraid of the microphone. Never fear. It is your friend. Be comfortable using the mike.

Our educational system has learned the importance of the

microphone and presenters can learn from the schools. A major study in classrooms across the country showed that when teachers wore tiny wireless microphones in class, students' behavior, attention, and performance improved. One researcher stated, "It should be standard equipment, based on these results." If it works for third-graders, it must be true for adults.

If you must speak from a lectern, move the stationary microphone before you begin to speak so it is close to your mouth. Then, orient all you say into that microphone. Move your eyes but not your head. It is your responsibility to speak into the microphone . . . it won't follow you.

One way to think about the microphone is to visualize a small fan inside of the microphone itself. The fan will either chop up your words or accelerate them, depending on the power of your voice. If you are soft-spoken in a microphone, you will be a slightly louder soft-spoken person on the receiving end. This is hardly a powerful presence. If you push those words past the "fan" inside the microphone, then the microphone will work for you and with you. You must use the microphone correctly; it will not work all by itself.

Maintain your comfort level with the microphone. Do not call attention to it by tapping on it, saying "Can you hear me now?" or by repeating "Testing, testing, test, test . . ." into the microphone when the audience is present. Get there early enough to make sure it works, to understand how it works, and to use it with comfort.

A lavalier mike is a small microphone that is attached with a clip to your shirt or suit collar near your chin and wired to a battery pack. If you have a lavalier, snake the wire through your clothing, clip the battery pack to your belt (professionals wear it in the small of their back), or to an inside pocket. Look in the mirror to make sure you have no dragging wires, as they are distracting to an audience and you if they snag on you.

A handheld microphone is also a possibility. This allows for you to moderate your voice depending on how close you hold it to your mouth. Standup comedians always use a handheld because they can whisper, explode, laugh, and generally do things that a lavalier microphone cannot help them do. One caution with a handheld. If you allow an audience member to speak into the microphone, never let go of it physically . . . you may not get it back! Always be in control so you can take it back when you need to.

Finally, during Q&A always repeat the question even if you think everyone heard it—not everyone did! And make sure you turn your microphone off whenever you are not speaking, on a break, in private conversations, or in the restroom.

The microphone can be a loyal friend if you treat it right.

49

You Own the Power of Performance

- **The role of connection powers great speeches.**
- **The role of emotion powers every presenter.**
- **The role of respect powers the audience.**

Content alone does not make a speech a memorable experience any more than food poorly presented makes for a great meal. On the other hand, when all you have is a flashy style and little content, you will leave your audience hungry and unsatisfied or, worse, angry and bitter for the lack of a memorable experience. When you talk too much at the expense of the audience hearing what you think, the audience can go away wondering how necessary you were.

While each of these elements is important when used in combination, they also point to a common misperception among new and experienced speakers alike. Performance is not just technique. Performance is not just perfect practice. Performance is more than the sum of the individual parts of a speech. Content, style, and interaction are certainly vital to a good presentation. If all you have, however, is those three things without performance, you will have only a good presentation, not a memorable one. Performance is much more.

Performance is the soul of the speech. When you walk away from a truly memorable play, concert, or movie and you have a "wow" feeling, it is then that you have witnessed a true performance. No longer is it simply a play with actors or a concert with a musician onstage. At these moments you have been drawn into a significant experience.

Think back to one of these times. What happened to you during that event? What made it so special for you? What did the performer, teacher, musician, or speaker do to elicit that response in you? They most likely added a touch of their soul to the mechanics of their work.

Listening to Yo-Yo Ma play the cello is an auditory experience. Watching Yo-Yo Ma play the cello is a real feast for the eyes and the ears. Listening to your favorite preacher or teacher is special, not only because of what they are doing, but more so because of what is happening inside of you while they are speaking.

Performance, or the soul of the speech, is your ability to understand the need of the audience to connect with you, not merely to communicate. Great speakers go even further: They look in the eyes of their audiences not only to establish a connection but also to stay with the audience in terms of pace, emotion, and experience. In the same way you look into the eyes of others grieving at a wake and pace yourself and your tone and your conversation to theirs. You look into their souls as best you can. Great speakers do the same thing. It is what happens inside of you and how you release that to your audience that is the central feature of the excellent speaker.

You succeed when you release a burning conviction of self-confidence, a deep respect for the audience, and an emotional connection to the content. Delivering a presidential address to the nation or a thirty-minute talk on a high school career day should be given with the same inner confidence and courage. While each occasion is different, to say one is less important than the other is a great and often committed error by even the best of speakers. It is not unimportant to those who decided to show up and to hear you. Taking the stage with confidence is deeply important for your performance. Confidence comes from you reminding yourself that even a "ten-minute update" is extremely vital to those present.

Respect for the audience is a key feature of the great speakers. The audience needs you, they want you, and they are your collaborators. When you understand that the audience is your social equal, then even your work with a group of five-year-olds will take on a new kind of significance. Kevin once watched a world-famous physician take an audience question with the comment, "Well, the question you should have asked is . . ." You can imagine how much interaction he had after that comment! More than silencing his audience, he was disrespectful to them. While they admired his content and his intelligence, they lost respect for him as a person in the process. Great speakers not only try to like their audiences and enjoy them but also respect the knowledge, power, and honor of working with that particular audience.

Great performance from the soul is an emotional connection. Watch any great entertainer or teacher and you will see deep emotional conviction to their material and your part in that. Songs, plays, movies, and speeches all have an emotional component that the speaker can choose to use or abuse. Even the most technical or scientific presentations need this emotional connection to be memorable.

COACH'S COMMENTS

Question: I certainly don't want to be too emotional, do I? I don't want to pander to the audience. Isn't it better and safer to just give them the facts and let them decide how they feel?

Your coach says: I agree that you don't want to abuse your audience by taking anything too far one way or the other. What you as a speaker often forget is just what you as an audience member are most wanting: a memorable experience with your speaker. How you do that will vary for each audience. Kevin worked for a "just the facts" client once who had little regard for interaction (none was allowed), PowerPoint slides had to be perfect and loaded with content, and time was vital; "don't dillydally" was the motto. This client was asking him to give up the soul of the performance! Kevin finally convinced him to encourage eye contact to connect the data with the audience as much as possible. It's a balancing act to give the audience what they need and a message that sticks.

50

Discover and Deliver Your Strengths

- **Know both sides of your personality for maximum presentation power.**
- **Let your strong side lead you to success.**
- **Power can be used over people or "with" others.**

Lead with your strengths, and don't fear your weaknesses. If you fixate on what you don't know or don't do well, you will never make progress—and it will show. At the same time, if you ignore your weaknesses, you will impede your progress.

Ignoring weakness may explain why some leaders are accused of being arrogant. They don't think they are arrogant, they think they are right. They don't check with their weaknesses, which are often just the flip side of their strengths. Assertive people can be aggressive. Friendly ones can become too accommodating. Thoughtful people can become too silent. These weaker traits can be evident in front of groups. Sadly, the presenter is often the last to know. Ineffective behavior repeats itself; audiences who aren't asked to evaluate don't, and communication never achieves its intent.

COACH'S COMMENTS

Your coach says: Whatever happens during your speech, stay in control. Never shout or lose your temper, never become sarcastic, never make an audience member look silly. Stay calm and in control. When some walk out of the room, focus on those who stayed. When you lose your place, don't get flustered; work to find your place. When the audience doesn't respond to your desire for a dialogue, move on. Stay in control and stay and sound powerful. Remember there is someone out there who thinks you are doing great, and you are helping them. Stay in control for them.

Carl Jung called it a "shadow side," the part in you that lingers in the background. Think of it as two sides of the same coin: One side sees daylight, and the other remains hidden but present nonetheless. Ask yourself the following questions:

- **Am I persuasive or manipulative?**
- **Am I cool under pressure or cold and insensitive to the needs of others?**
- **Am I concerned with accuracy or am I a demanding perfectionist?**
- **Do I care for the feelings of others or am I a superpleaser?**
- **Do I want the job done or do I want to look good?**

The fact of the matter is you probably are all of these things from time to time. Awareness is the key. One of our coaching clients had a reputation (and a strength) for quickly sizing up people. He could also assess situations, analyze challenges, and understand what plan of action was required . . . all in a relatively short period of time. This served him well as a presenter, usually. He handled objections beautifully; he quickly sized up an audience member's comments and even hidden agendas. He skillfully paraded the correct facts and statistics for the right buyers.

However, as you can imagine, one of his greatest weaknesses was seen as being "too quick" and "too fast" with people as well as with situations. When he was right, he was right on. When wrong, he was very wrong. Being very wrong for a major presentation was not a good thing.

Another one of our clients who developed an important under-standing of this strength/weakness dynamic admitted at one meeting: "I wanted to react like I always would have. Instead, I stayed quiet and asked more questions. It wasn't easy. I knew that I knew." When he was asked what made the difference for him, he said: "I knew that my group didn't yet know. That reminded me I had to do more than just know better than them; I had to listen better to them."

This leader learned he could use his strengths. He just had to not use them so quickly, especially when others were involved in the decision making. He listened visibly in front of groups. He listened verbally and visually during Q&A sessions. He worked hard to paraphrase, repeat words, and review ideas; this slowed him down and reminded him of others' styles. Using your strengths makes all the difference. The presenter who understands this takes an important step in his or her relationships with others—before, during, and after the presentation.

Be careful: Your greatest strengths can yield to your greatest weaknesses.

Part VIII

Master Interaction

51

Walk a Fine Line When Facilitating

- **Don't dump data on your audience.**
- **Facilitating is one of the most effective strategies you can utilize as a speaker.**
- **Strive for interaction.**

Our downfall as professionals is seldom caused by a lack of information about the latest techniques in marketing, finance, or production. Rather it comes because of a lack of an interpersonal skill, a failure to get the best out of the people who possess the necessary information.
—Kets de Vries, author and professor

COACH'S COMMENTS

Question: I've been asked to facilitate a meeting. Does this mean I have to have some clear opinions up front, just in case?

Your coach says: When you facilitate, no one really cares what you think. This is difficult for smart presenters to accept, but it is true nonetheless. Stay at the flipchart and encourage the discussion. If you must contribute, do so at the end in a way that summarizes and encourages everyone else's contribution. "I have heard you say you are concerned about three things . . ." is an effective way to begin to wrap up the discussion. When you facilitate, what you think is less important than what they think.

The days of dumping data on audiences are coming to a very abrupt end. The presenter who knows this and who adapts to it will be the victor. Today's audiences are evolving into a more sophisticated group of people who appreciate an active facilitated meeting rather than a passive speaker-listener format. The more common facilitated meetings become, the more audiences are going to demand them, and grow impatient when they are spoken *at* instead of *with*.

You can be on the cutting edge of this trend by developing your facilitation skills until they become a normal and relaxed part of your dynamic during presentations. You will be regarded with more trust, understood to be a better listener, and your ability to influence will increase exponentially.

One challenge for a group of corporate scientists was how to facilitate conversations with customers rather than simply presenting or dumping data on them. When facilitating information is done well, it is the most effective thing a company can do to inform customers about the drugs, the scientific developments, and the advances available to them. Later, during meetings, the scientists were able to convince their peers to speak with one another, reach consensus, and interact with the lay CEO or CFO. They saw firsthand that these new skills pay off in a very big way.

How often have you sat at a meeting hour after hour and not been asked for your opinion? How often have you been expected to follow along in a workbook of printed-out PowerPoint slides as the presenter read each one from the screen? How about the times when the presenter and one attendee decided that they would either spend the meeting verbally jousting with one another or acting like two good ol' boys with one another at the expense of everyone else in attendance? These types of meetings are terribly ineffective and unnecessary.

Mastering a positive facilitation style is one of the most important skills for a professional communicator.

52

Always Remember: It's About Them

- **The experience is what an audience wants and needs.**
- **It will help your presentation to involve the audience.**
- **Let them speak to you about the topic.**

Remember, the quality and the impact of your presentations will make your career. Many presenters think it is their content that drives audience satisfaction. This is a mistake. It is the experience that drives the audience. It is also the experience that makes you a memorable feature of that presentation.

In order for this to happen, you need to not only be a great presenter, but you also need to be able to facilitate—to involve your audience. There are three primary ways to facilitate:

- **Suggest.** You are far better to say: "I would like to suggest that you consider XYZ" than by saying, "It is clear beyond a doubt that XYZ . . ." When presenters act as though what they are saying is true, it places them in a difficult position with the audience who then has to judge whether they are right or not. If, the presenter "suggests" something for the audience, then the audience member is internally thinking not about truth, but rather about possibility.

- **Question.** Effective facilitators lace their presentations and their discussions with good questions. "As I present this segment for the next ten minutes, I'd like you to consider question XYZ." Or: "In your clinical experience, what are the three greatest risks associated with XYZ?" Questions involve the audience. Ask only one question, and then become expectantly silent. Look as though you expect an answer, because you do. And you will get one!

- **Review.** This can be one of the highest forms of facilitation. Here the presenter guides the audience through their own learning. When we teach at the university, we usually draw three interlocking circles and label each one with a point that we want to make. Then we step back and ask what this says to each student. Or we will ask what is missing, what is wrong, what could be labeled better. Discussion always ensues.

COACH'S COMMENTS

Question: How can I avoid the feeling that I'll mess up and people won't take me seriously?

Your coach says: Always remember your customer—what is it that they want to do, feel, think, change as a result of your work? They don't care about your topic unless it helps them and solves their problems. They don't understand your topic the way you do. You have to translate the title and your presentation topic into language that is meaningful to them, not only to you. What does the title of your presentation say about them? Don't make it about you or your interest—make it relevant to them.

The title needs to say to them what the presentation is, what it can do for them, and what problems they won't have because of it. Try going to the bookstore and look at titles. Notice how little time it takes to make an impression on you! The same is true for your audience—they will give you a little more time, but not much.

The first four minutes of your talk especially need to do the same thing. Grab their attention by speaking about them, not about you. It is always about them!

Facilitation is your ability to involve the audience in a dialogue with you and with one another. Throughout your presentation and the discussion, summarize what individuals and/or groups have said. Sometimes this highlights gray areas that require further discussion. Other times, summarizing works as a transition into the next part of the presentation. You can also use rhetorical questions to segue into a new topic.

Every facilitator determines his or her own comfort level and estimates the value of discussions or arguments to the overall exchange of ideas. If people are becoming so animated that they talk over one another and the atmosphere begins to resemble a circus, the moderator will need to make adjustments, assert more control, and establish the polite norm of "one person at a time."

Don't be afraid to take control, but do so with a light touch. Professionals are very aware of being talked down to. When they fight with one another or you sense you are losing control, simply step up to the task and say something like: "I hear three things today." Then step to the flipchart and start writing. The audience will listen to you and you can come across as knowledgeable, a listener, and as someone who can make things better.

Always be wary of coming across too heavy-handed: "I'm in charge here!" Too much control flattens the enthusiasm and willingness of an audience to both listen and exchange ideas. Also beware of coming across like the stereotype of a classroom teacher. "I want you all to stop talking to one another and look up here" is not a way to speak to adults, although many inexperienced presenters try it—once! It will make them hate you . . . a lot!

It is a fine line, but one you will conquer with practice, preparation, and attention to details—especially details about your audience members. What they focus on plays a vital role in how your presentation flows. Don't ignore their concerns.

If you work your audience and their needs into your material, you will gain their confidence and they will work right along with you.

**THREE THINGS TO DO WHEN THE AUDIENCE DOESN'T
SEEM TO BE WITH YOU**

- **Ask yourself "why?"** Are you going over time, do they
  need a break, do you know them well enough?

- **Take action.** Speed up or slow down as needed. Do whatever
  you can to vary whatever you were doing.

- **Involve the audience.** Break them into groups of three (no
  larger) and give them a question to discuss for four minutes.
  Then ask for a report, use the flipchart, and discuss. This will
  almost always revive a tired audience. (When breaking them
  into threes, just say, "When I give you the signal, I want you to
  get into groups of three—but not with anyone sitting next to you
  or near you. OK, everyone, up and into groups of three." This is
  not anywhere near as risky as it may sound. Get them physically
  moving and talking—and they will think you are a brilliant
  presenter!)

53

Become "Learner-Centric"

- What the audience learns is your only concern.
- The audience will learn more than you have given them.
- Your value to the meeting planner is what the audience learns.

St. Augustine, the Catholic saint who lived a very wild life in his youth, wrote "Love God, and do as you will." Upon first reading this, it sounds great, especially for many younger people! Upon closer reading, what he conveyed was how all-encompassing and how complete a life we live when we love God. In effect, for him, loving God requires that we live a certain way. There are ways to live that are in harmony and ways that are not in harmony. For him, it all starts with one premise.

We don't know if Augustine was a compelling speaker. We do know he was a good writer. And as such, he was certainly "reader-centric." He knew how to grab and hold on to his readers' attention and teach with content. Speakers can learn from the fact that the premise he began with was rich with meaning. It could be read and reread, and its meaning would persist and deepen.

COACH'S COMMENTS

Your coach says: There is literally nothing else in this book as important as being centered on your audience. If you understand this concept, you will have it all. If you do not understand this idea, nothing you do will truly impact others in a substantial way. It's a concept

often overlooked because it comes last—after the presentation—
when the average presenter breathes a sigh of relief and tucks it
away in a file. The above-average presenter knows otherwise.
Therefore, spend time speaking with those you spoke to. Ask them
what they learned, what they found most valuable, and how they
will implement what they heard. Some call this "listening to the market" and it is a very good thing to do. Don't focus on what you
wanted them to learn, focus on what they said they learned. Then
adjust as needed.

**When you, like St. Augustine, begin with a simple premise
that is rich with meaning, you become learner-centric.** To arrive
at a good premise, think: What is most useful for this audience?
What notion or phrase could they take away from this presentation
that would have a lasting effect for them? What is something they
could hold on to as they remember what they learned this day?

Sales trainers often use the phrase, "Customers justify with
logic, but they buy with emotion." Motivational speakers say,
"People don't care how much you know until they know how
much you care." Writers of books like this one say, "The flipchart
is your friend!" These are simple premises. It is only with time
and experience that you begin to understand the depth of the
truth of these short statements.

**When you are learner-centric, everything you do revolves
around the learner.** Establishing your content becomes important,
but it is only the start. Securing the environment of the room and
the audiovisuals is an important next (and ongoing) step. Then
comes the real magic that is no magic at all. It is the hard work
of thinking about how to teach so that the learners learn. Ask
yourself:

• What will be the organizing phrase or principle or premise of
your presentation?

• How have you organized the flow of your remarks? What sections or subsections will you use?

- What open-ended questions will you be asking? Do you have them written down?

- When will you use the flipchart?

- When do you want some discussion by the participants and how will you ask them for it?

- What are your three main goals for this meeting? (This is a critical part of every presentation, and we recommend this be the first and last thing you think about.)

When you are learner-centric, you will do certain things for the audience that other presenters fail to do. Learners love positive attention from the teacher, so you will thank contributors, show your appreciation for being with them, and consider it an honor to work with this group. They will feel special because you really consider them special.

Learners also love to be stimulated beyond what they thought when they came in the door. Again, in a positive way, a learner-centric presenter will think about how to stimulate new ideas, a fresh approach, even some bit of surprise for the learners. One sales speaker begins his program with this statement: "I am not here to teach you anything. You don't have to change a bit. Training sales people to do new things is not what we are here for today. So relax!" Then, with a wry grin, he adds: "I am only here to remind you of what once made you successful and to inspire you to do it again . . . because it will be easy money for you and the company."

Learners love to respond openly as long as they don't feel foolish in front of the group. Save them in front of the group, no matter what they do. Kevin always asks his audience members to use their cell phones in a special area, outside the door. Once a physician attendee answered a call and continued her conversation in the middle of class in the second row! No matter what Kevin thought (!), what he did was catch her eye and quietly say, "You can use the cell phone area." The doctor nodded and continued with the call. Kevin had already launched into his topic, so he continued to talk, walked right in front of the "phone physician," waited for a pause or an audience laugh, and then touched the doctor on the shoulder and said, "Thank you for taking your call out there," motioning to the hallway. She looked a bit startled, got up, and went outside. Others nearby laughed and gave a look that conveyed, "How stupid is that person!" Kevin purposely said to them, "Easy to do . . . happened to me last week!"

Learner-centric presenters are known for their enthusiasm. If you can't be visibly excited about your topic, there is no reason in the world they should. Enthusiasm is critical for your success—and for their success, too! Move around the room, keep them guessing what will be next, enjoy the audience, have fun, keep hammering away at your three major points, ask open-ended questions, and watch their eyes and their involvement.

Learner-centric presenters care about their audience. When someone sneezes, they say "God bless you." When someone is shivering, they ask if the room temperature is too cold. When a question is asked, they always repeat the question. The audience then feels as though they are being taken care of, cared for, and cared about. And you'll be cared for later, in the form of higher evaluations!

**You can be focused on yourself or on them,
but your success resides with them.**

54

Technical Experts Are People Too

- **Technical presentations do not have to be boring.**
- **The best technical presenters communicate their passion.**
- **Connect with elegant simplicity.**

Do you remember dissecting a frog in biology? Most people do. Do you remember any of the lectures about dissection? Most people don't. They remember what the frog looked like, smelled like, even what it felt like. They don't remember much about the innards. Experience creates vivid memories. Technical experts who can engage the experience, rather than just expose people to the data, succeed as presenters.

How can you create vivid pictures of technically sophisticated data? There are many ways to do this without PowerPoint slides. Create an experience, communicate your passion, and involve your listeners through connection and clarity.

Create an experience to connect. As much as possible, encourage and invite the listener to experience your excitement. Be the cheerleader for the technology. For example, we coached a highly capable electronics engineer who was planning a presentation on the latest microphone technology for the marketing team. He opened his talk by playing music the twentysomething-year-old team would relate to, using several different formats. This positioned him to advise them on marketing the current products for the iPod and MP3 user. He was talking their language before he talked his engineering language.

Communicate your passion about the technology. Most technical pros care deeply about their topics but it's often difficult for the audience to see or hear it. The passion gets upstaged behind a monotone delivery and too many slides. Communicating your passion is not as difficult as you might think. You don't have to be an actor. You can be yourself, but jumpstart your energy level. Everyone who loves his or her work communicates passion in some way, and everyone is a technical expert at something.

It is the gifted presenter and the prepared presenter who works to communicate his or her passion. Some do it with humor. One scientist read a formula and technical specifications as if he were reading both an Italian menu and a romantic novel. Afterward he paused, wiped his brow with a handkerchief, looked at the audience, and said, "Whew, it don't get no better than that!" Some are more direct. One pharmacist said, "I have some very exciting research to speak about today." She did it with life in her eyes because, for her, it really was exciting.

Work diligently to connect and involve your listeners. Think concertedly about your listener's needs. Make it easy for your audience to learn. If you've ever been in the audience when it was obvious the speaker wasn't connecting, you know it is an excruciating experience. As an audience member, you become uncomfortable, embarrassed, bored, and sometimes angry. This doesn't have to happen, but it is up to you to prevent it from happening. Do your homework. Make some phone calls, get feedback, and talk to your manager. Find out several ways you can connect immediately. Work to establish your commonality. Talk with people as they enter.

COACH'S COMMENTS

Question: I'm making my first technical presentation and want to make a good impression. What is the best way to do this?

Your coach says: When you are an expert in something, don't say that you are. Let your introducer do that. Carry a biographical description of yourself that they can refer to. Some carry an entire word-for-word introduction. Others use bullet points; still others use a simple paragraph. Note here that, again, shorter is better! Also, don't be afraid to get personal. The introducer can mention that you won the Nobel Prize, have three doctorates, and just invented a cure for cancer. What will warm the audience is that you know how to skateboard, have eight children, or was a spelling bee champion in fourth grade! Always end with that or use it as your opening line. Then let your expertise show through what you say about your subject, not what you say about yourself.

It is critical you connect early. Too often, we watch presenters make the mistake of thinking if they talk more they will connect better. When you feel offtrack and like you are not connecting, stop! Put the audience into small groups of two or three and give them a question to respond to. Use a generic question that will always elicit a response:

- **What has been the most challenging part of being an XYZ in the past year?**

- **If you could summarize your role this past week in one word, what would it be?**

Then give them a few minutes to discuss, go to the flipchart, and work the group from there. If you have a PowerPoint program, touch the "B" key once to blank out your slide so it won't distract. Bring it back to the screen by hitting the "B" key again. When you are in trouble, don't make it worse by going on and on and on. The audience has the connection if only you will let them talk.

Be very clear about what you do. "I can't explain what I do," a consultant once said to a sales trainer at a sales conference. The sales trainer, not mincing any words, said, "Then get out of the business." The technical person should remember this, too. You can be the best technical expert in your field, but if you can't communicate the value of your work or the results of your work, you shouldn't be the one speaking!

Or you can get clear! Talk to your friends, family, your dry cleaner, and your minister, and get very clear so you can learn to communicate what you do with elegant simplicity. Elegant simplicity is not "dumbing down," but rather teaching in a sophisticated way at the highest of levels. When a pharmaceutical professional says, "This is a very good drug," and then moves to the research, she is making a strong persuasive statement—although she is using very simple language.

Being clear only comes from practice and rehearsal. If you can describe what you want so that your former college roommate who became an actor can understand, then you are a teacher par excellence! Then you are clear.

Technical should never be complicated. You never impress others with your complexity. Use elegant simplicity instead.

55

Be Prepared with Questions

- **Preparation is the key to asking good questions.**
- **Good questions help the audience think.**
- **Good questions also help the presenter see how the audience is thinking.**

Open-ended questions can be lifesavers. Consider your personal relationships with teenagers and how conversations hinge on the details: "How was school today?" is a question that will elicit an "okay" or a noncommittal shrug of the shoulders. "Tell me about your day" may still get a rolling of the eyes, but it opens up the question and allows a possible answer about anything and everything. "How did you feel when the teacher did that?" is more likely to elicit a personal response.

Adults aren't much different. Asking the appropriate open-ended question during a meeting provides you with a powerful tool. Likewise, a close-ended question is unforgiving. "What do you think of the material we covered in today's discussion?" begs for a "liked it didn't," shrugging-shoulders type of answer. But "what was the most helpful section of the presentation today?" entices listeners to offer an opinion; it flatters their innermost analyst and gives them a chance to contribute.

Researchers at the University of Pennsylvania did a study many years ago contrasting the way waiters and waitresses speak with us after our meal has been served. "Everything OK?" is the traditional question from a waiter. Sometimes the customer even lies just to move things along. But what if your waitress said:

"What is the one thing I could have done to make this meal more pleasurable for you?" You would probably be more inclined to answer with the truth. The study also found that those who used the open-ended questions also received the higher tips! And they should get more money. They are allowing their guests to say whatever they want, to reach down deep and offer up any real concerns.

> ### COACH'S COMMENTS
>
> **Your coach says:** Some presenters use questions at the beginning of their presentation to focus the audience's attention. Some have open-ended questions (which they have written down and rehearsed) and use them for audience interaction and discussion. In any event, use questions to organize, stimulate, or even to conclude your presentation. You don't ever have to have all the answers when presenting. But you do have to leave the audience excited, stimulated, thoughtful, and wanting more. Then you'll be asked back!

Even better for sparking summary discussion is a specific targeted question, such as: "How do you feel the information we presented today might impact your work this coming week when you are back in the office?" If a recorder can write the answers down on a flipchart, everyone will benefit from this even more detailed discussion of the day's information.

When you direct the audience to questions that are close-ended, you diminish discussion and overall focus. Audiences respond as we set them up to respond. Utilize open-ended questions to clarify gray areas and leave the audience with a firmer grasp of the materials covered.

Consider writing these conversation starters on a 4×6 card that you will carry into the meeting when you are facilitating:

- **Tell me how . . .**
- **What is the most/best/least . . . ?**
- **In what ways . . . ?**

- **Can you give me an example in your clinical experience of a patient who . . . ?**

- **How does this research match your own experience . . . ?**

- **Please give an example of . . . ?**

- **What is the rationale for . . . ?**

- **What are three things you want this procedure to do . . . ?**

- **What do these numbers say about . . . ?**

Avoid dead-end questions that stall your audience interaction:

- **Does that make sense?**

- **Is anybody worried?**

- **Do you agree?**

- **Seem right?**

- **Who's the only one who answered "A" on the quiz?**

- **Anyone want to own up to that one?**

- **Any other questions?**

- **What do you think, I mean, do you agree, I mean I think that it could be this or that . . .**

Remember to rehearse your questions, write them down, and carry them with you. Presenters who write down their questions in advance are called . . . successful!

Professionals are not spontaneous. Rehearsal is a professional activity. The paradox is that when you are well rehearsed, you will be able to better handle the spontaneous times. Keep questions short, open-ended, and targeted to the topic. Do not ask a question and then keep going on and on and on with further clarifications

of the question. Watch Larry King interviews. He asks a question
and shuts up.

Say it and shut up . . . but have an expectant look on your face.
Put the pressure on them. Wait for an answer—there is a weak
link in every audience! Kevin spoke to a group of seventy doctors
once and they were extremely quiet when he asked them questions. He resorted to threats. "I will wait," he said to them, smiling. Sure enough, he found his weak link who got the ball rolling.
Actually your "weak link" is your bravest audience member. Treasure that person!

**Ask one simple open-ended question, be quiet . . .
and look expectant.**

56

Become a Master Teacher

- **Don't merely teach; become a master at explaining.**
- **Expert doesn't mean "easy to understand."**
- **A master teacher focuses on his or her audience.**

The best way to learn anything is to teach it. Reading, researching, and even knowing are very different than communicating for understanding. See yourself as a master teacher with every presentation you give.

Too often when we present we think of ourselves as experts. We are experts, of course, but we should not believe our own advertising. That wrongheaded approach often befalls other experts; it's an attitude that says, "The audience should come to me." We then rely on lecture as the only means of communicating.

FROM THE PROS

"The principal thing I've learned over time is to relax. This means don't try to do too much, don't overdo it with too much stuff, be natural, and have fun. For my first public speech, I spoke to a crowd of lawyers at the annual intellectual property conference at the John Marshall Law School in 1987.

"I had about an hour to speak but prepared enough material for about five hours. I didn't cover it all, of course, and what I did cover I rushed. I had no time to relate to the audience. I was tied to pages and pages of notes. I was glued to the podium. Over time, I've moved to trying to do less, and as a result can do more. I'm more relaxed, better able to connect with the audience, free of piles of notes, free from the podium. And get better audience reaction."

—Mark, copyright attorney

In the scientific community, for example, this is widespread, accepted, and unfortunate. Often, we have heard scientists come out of a meeting lauding the expert for her knowledge, but shaking their heads out of boredom or frustration. Experts tend to rely on superior knowledge. Many experts are teachers with superior knowledge. They just aren't master teachers.

Sometimes we see ourselves as celebrities. We may be famous in our own right or in this local community or with this audience. There is certainly nothing wrong with enjoying our fifteen minutes of fame. But banish that attitude as soon as you open your mouth to speak. Celebrities speak adoringly of themselves. Famous master teachers are concerned with the audience.

Other times we feel "less than" those in the audience, like we are the ones who need to learn more. Perhaps you are a layperson in front of a sea of physicians, an employee facing colleagues with years more experience, or a citizen confronting a panel of legislators. It is too easy in these situations to allow your fear and your insecurity to blur your message.

But what if you remind yourself to focus? What if you remember to teach them the very information they wanted from you? What if you knew and shared with them the essence of what they most needed to know? Then you have conquered your fears and accomplished your mission—to share information with your audience in an intelligent and also accessible way. "Regret and fear are the twin thieves that rob us of today," a wise person once said. Don't be motivated by either.

Focused master teachers remind themselves that they are important for a special reason to this particular audience.

COACH'S COMMENTS

Your coach says: Endings and outcomes are what presentations are all about. There is really only one reason you were asked to give the presentation you just gave—some change in the attendees was needed. It could be a change of information, action, follow-up, skill development, or something else. We have all heard the following: "Begin with the end in mind." "Show your last slide first." "Write the title after you wrote the book or article." Or as one direct marketer says: "Write the ad for your product before you develop the product itself!" What all of this advice has in common are outcomes, benefits, and endings. Master teachers are concerned with outcomes—what will the student *do, know,* and *be* as a result of their time together. When you spend preparation time on these three questions—What should the audience do? What should they know to do that? What should they be?—you will indeed be in a position to teach masterfully.

57

Know the Nuances of Learners' Needs and Wants

Coach's Comments

This is such an important topic that the coach wants to weigh in quickly. Learners have needs and wants, as does any audience. They may not always know their needs; many times it's up to you to figure that out. They do, however, know their wants; they often know precisely what they want. If you satisfy their needs and neglect their wants, you'll have given them the spinach without the bacon dressing. It is good for them, but unlikely to be ordered again. Knowing the difference between needs and wants is the mark of a pro. Therefore it is essential to consider the following questions as you approach your learners:

- **What does this group want and what do they *really* want?**

- **What do they need that they know that they need and expect of you?**

- **What is the hidden need that is vital to their success?**

- **Finally, what do *you* want and need from them?**

What the group *says* they want and what they *really* want is an emotional issue for most audiences. We often hear audiences say prior to the speech, "I hope she's as good as she was last time." Or they'll say to one another, "What have you heard about him? Is he any good?" Or the classic, "I hope this isn't going to be a waste of time. I hope it's not going to be boring." Like it or not, audiences want to be entertained, informed, and emotionally satisfied before, during, and after your speech. As we have mentioned before, you'll have about four minutes, your first four minutes, to assure and reassure them. Therefore, give them the meat of the matter right away. Don't waste time with "Great to be here, thank you for having me, I'm so-and-so with such-and-such a degree." Get to the meat—their meat—immediately and put them on notice that you are someone who knows what they need and what they really need.

If you're speaking to the printing industry, for example, start with the meat of the matter for them, perhaps like this: "The printing industry has never been at such a crossroad before. And for those of us using the gravure method, we too are at a crossroad, except ours is on top of a cliff. Our choices this year, our choices together, will either keep us together or will accelerate our fall. Today, I will outline three things to ensure you and yours will stay on top."

What the audience needs and what they know they need are both important and often different. For example, sales audiences know they need motivation, so they hire motivational speakers. They also know that they cannot remember the name of last year's motivational speaker! Want to be different? Speak to their real needs—application to their experience and your own with memorable tips to implement these ideas. When you are tempted to go on and on about you, stop! If you have preinterviewed some of them, you can easily go on and on about *them*. Knowing this, you had better be prepared to meet that burning need head on. The need to apply experience may not be at the top of their minds, but it will be at the top of your success as a speaker.

Imagine you're addressing a customer service group. They may tell you about a need for satisfied repeat customers. However, a hidden need vital to the success of customer service agents goes deeper than the skills of how to talk on the phone. It is also the attitude they carry when confronted with anger, rage, or fear. Helping them access that inner attitude will go a long way in helping them understand the hidden need that may interfere or may help them succeed in what can be a very difficult job.

Finally, what do you want and need from them? Why is this an important question? The answer will color your presentation from beginning to end—from the first words you write. Do you want to establish something? Do you want to create an experience, an impression, or an outcome? Teachers at a university often want their semester classes to form a kind of small community or team in addition to the content of the class. Preachers often want the congregation to talk back while they are speaking with an occasional "Amen" to keep things on track. Politicians want to be interrupted with applause. What do you want? You may want simple nods saying, "I'm with you," or lots of questions, or note taking, or laughter. Do you want them to sign on the dotted line? Do you want them to challenge your thinking? Be honest and clear about what you want.

The nuances of both speaker and audience needs and wants color the tone and the outcome of any presentation.

Part IX

Follow Up for More

Build Upon the Audience Perception of Your Expertise Before, During, and After Your Speech

One of the powerful things about speaking, even informally, is the expertise that the audience gives you. Even when they disagree with you, the audience perceives that you have a right and an expertise to share with them.

We have discussed the importance of up-front positioning earlier in this book: In your communication with the audience prior to your presentation, give them something that tells them who you are and why you are their presenter. Professionals do this in their phone calls and e-mail interviews as well as in the introduction to the audience. This helps the audience answer the question, "Who is this?" The sooner they can answer this question, the sooner they will be ready to listen. We mention it again here because it positions your follow-up, too.

During your speech, make sure that you back up your statistics with sources, data, and research. Be precise here and you will help your audience hear you better and they will have the opportunity to follow up as they wish. You can ask for their follow-up within your speech, if appropriate. You can encourage follow-up with stories and examples of what previous audience members have done. Annotated handouts are helpful and Web sites, links to articles, free brochures, and other suggestions for more reading or connection. You are readying your follow-up with each step.

After the speech, be ready. You need to be ready to proactively call, e-mail, or simply respond to offer help. One meeting planner that Kevin worked with asked the presenters—many famous in their field—to be available to answer any e-mailed questions for one week following their presentations. It is unlikely they were deluged, but the offer was well received by the audience. Those who needed that kind of follow-up had the opportunity.

Follow-up is something that a lot of people say they do, but few really do.

The Eyes of the Audience Will Help You Follow Up

- **Follow-up begins as you speak.**
- **The audience is central to success.**
- **Audience eyes don't lie.**

Follow-up is often seen as an after-the-fact, after-the-speech activity. Effective follow-up really begins by watching your audience as you speak. You have interviewed them, you have customized your presentation, you are addressing their challenges, and you are using good presentation techniques. There is only one more thing you need to do as you present—watch.

Watch any audience and you will notice the clues to your success and to what they need after the speech. You can even watch audiences that you are a part of. If you observe faces, sense body tension, watch note taking or side whispers, you will capture many clues to the places of greatest meaning in the message. Be an audience student in order to find out what is in the minds, the hearts, and—most important—the expectations of the audience. Audience members will often come up after a presentation, feeling that the speech content was directed just to them. How many times have you felt the same in a religious ceremony? Somehow the minister, the priest, or the rabbi knew! What they were really doing was using their vast experience for watching and getting ready for follow-up. A priest, rabbi, or minister is always ready for follow-up. It's an integral, expected part of their jobs. What if speakers approached every talk the same way—with absolute follow-up in mind?

Inexperienced speakers will focus on their words, their slides, and their plans rather than auidence clues for success. By now, you have gathered that we have made the audience a central theme in this book. What seems like common sense—that the audience is central to success—is often ignored, and that is the major reason for speaker failure.

When you watch the eyes of the audience, you can use four primary indicators that will help you gauge your effectiveness and guide your follow-up:

- **First, notice those who are smiling and seem eager to connect with you.** These are your primary encouragers and you want to identify them early and often throughout your program. They are doing their job for you and you can feed off their energy in doing your job for them. To follow up with them, compliment their involvement and ask what more you can do for them.

- **Then, look for those who are watching you without much expression and make contact with them when you say something of importance.** Use a nod, a shift of your eyebrows, always with a smile, however slight. This sends the message to them that they have a role to play. In a sense you are converting a possible judge and critic into a possible encourager and learner. To follow up, find out if you connected. Get to know them better; perhaps continue to work on the relationship in other ways: coffee chats, e-mail reports, testimonials, or helpful and unexpected information.

- **When you see the audience interacting with one another, this is an opportunity to remind yourself that your words are being translated.** Nods, laughs, turns of the head are all good signs that the audience is enjoying what you just said or at least they have been provoked to more thought by it. In this case, you can select to comment afterward one on one; for example, "Joe, I noticed your reaction to the market strategy comments.

Did I hit the right note? Was there something that you related to in particular?"

- **When you use highly emotional words, strong words, or definitive language, make strong eye contact with a variety of audience members and keep the eye contact with them for a moment longer than usual.** These are also called pregnant words. They are vital to any speech and need to be emphasized. Consider this example: "McDonald's didn't even have salads as recently as *five years ago*. [Wait a moment and look to connect.] To date we have sold over three hundred *million salads*. [Wait and look.] Can you imagine what *the next five years will bring*? [Wait and look.]" Simply reading these statistics without connecting does not convey the importance, the impressiveness, and the amazement of the numbers. The eyes do.

As emphasized in chapter 33, eye contact is important for any speaker. The eye contact we speak of here is that of a highly advanced level. With this skill, the speaker is "watching the watching" of the audience.

Eyes are the windows to the soul of your audience and to the impact of your performance.

60

Ask for the Right Kinds of Information

- **Prioritize and select information.**
- **All information is not helpful.**
- **Information about how your audience thinks is key.**

Information can help you. Throughout this book, we have advocated that information is your friend (as is the audience, the microphone, and the audiovisual help at your location). Information is your vital link to an audience you do not yet know. It is a link to the outcomes your client most wants you to know. It is also your link to the presentation you have not yet given to this particular audience for this unique client. Information helps.

Information can also hurt you. If you spend too much time gathering information, you will miss the "people information" vital to your success. In the same way advertising is not written with the best grammar in mind (on purpose), and in the same way the spoken word is quite different from the written word, so too information is not always helpful information.

Spend too much time on the company's Web site and you will risk sounding like a corporate parrot. Spend too much time talking to the wrong people and you'll begin to sound like them. This is especially important for those of you who are detail-oriented. Typically, the more details you have, the more confident you feel. But remember: More is not always better.

Try thinking about information in the following ways—useful versus useless, helpful versus unhelpful, and productive

versus stagnating. When you see information in these ways, you will appreciate and glimpse the world of the audience from the inside out rather than as the outsider looking in. Seen this way, Web site information by and large is really only background information for a presenter in order to create credibility when specific terms are mentioned or basic information is needed. What a presenter really needs from the Web site is not there—what is life like for this audience? This is the key to a superior presentation. The Web site will tell you how the sales territories are divided up regionally. What it will hint at, if you look carefully, is how this division affects the individual salesperson who has to travel that territory.

Seeing the world from the inside out gives you a dose of reality that is always useful. To get that dose of reality, ask wise people good questions. Their answers will take you quickly from useless to useful. Chris, a twenty-eight-year food industry veteran we know, helped us visualize how experienced fast-food managers reinforce store goals. He said, "You can have each shifts' goals written on a piece of paper in the store, and team leaders can initial those goals when completed. But, you still need to be in the store frequently listening, observing, and checking on customers to make sure that what's on paper is really happening. It's not an issue of trust; it's an issue of training and development. An experienced manager knows to look beyond the initials on the goal sheet."

When you interview selected audience members about their lives, make sure you ask extensional questions, such as, "Can you tell me a little more about how that affects your sales? Family life? Future of the company? Competition?" Ask hypothetical, thought-provoking questions, such as, "Just between you and me, what do you think would happen if you didn't have weekly teleconferences with the team?" Or you could ask, "I know the sales force is supposed to be on the road four times a week, but can you think of any improvements to the system that would be more productive and perhaps less rigid for the sales force?"

Finding the answers to these questions starts people thinking and, more important, it opens a window into their thinking for you. Work to understand their thinking, and you have the keys to their behavior. Work only on their behavior and you'll be disrupted and derailed by their thinking every time. As the presenter you are in a unique position to bring out the important information and use it to meet the outcomes. No host can really do this. Only an outsider or an "inside outsider" can do this by virtue of you presenting to all assembled at once.

COACH'S COMMENTS

Your coach says: It is always OK to get personal with your presentation as long as the audience sees it as for them, and not only about you. Be careful here. This sounds very easy but it is not. Many a speaker gets very carried away with "speaker hormones." The pros often use a "show of hands" technique to involve the audience in answering easy, light questions. For example, "How many of you experience stress?" is a great question to unify and personalize. Nearly everyone feels some stress, no matter his or her level or type of work.

The late Johnny Carson always advocated the rule of three when telling his jokes. He saved the best for last. Therefore it is helpful to ask two questions: "How many of you experience stress? How many of you notice others when they experience stress?" Next, pause for a moment. Then have a lighter, funnier "third" comment: "How many of you notice when others have stress only when they are around you?"

This is why they asked you to present. You have the ability and the platform to help them with their thinking. You can influence, persuade, stimulate, and motivate them to do something different.

**The reason you are presenting and no one else was
selected is because you know how to use information
you get from your audience.**

61

Get Immediate Feedback

- **Don't fear feedback, and don't take it too seriously, either.**
- **When you focus on outcomes and not your popularity, you can read evaluations more objectively.**
- **Strive to simplify.**

Listen before, during, and after your presentations. Ahead of time, phone some of the audience members and ask them what they would like to learn. Ask for their greatest challenges. Ask for their burning questions. Do the same during your presentation. Engage in a dialogue whenever you can.

Ask for written evaluations for every one of your presentations. Read them thoroughly. Eliminate the top 10 percent as well as the bottom 10 percent (some will always like you and others will always hate you!). Find at least one idea in every stack of evaluations you can use to change, modify, or improve your presentation. Master teachers who are learner-centric prepare as well as listen to feedback.

When you focus on outcomes and not your popularity, you can read evaluations more objectively. Outcomes have to do with the learner, not just with you. Frame your evaluation questions to reflect what your audience has learned and not just whether they liked you or enjoyed the program.

COACH'S COMMENTS

Question: I'd like to be better at asking people what they think right after my talk, but I'm so keyed up at that point, I don't know what to say. Any ideas?

Your coach says: In addition to asking those who compliment you after your talk with "What especially did you like?" there are other ways to find out how you impacted others. Ask! "Before we finish, I'd like each of you to pick one word that describes what you learned or 'relearned' today" is another great way to elicit answers that give you vital information and help the audience receive some important information as well.

Some of the following questions can be helpful to audiences in evaluating their learning and your program:

- **What did you learn today that was most helpful to you?**

- **Please give an example of how it will be helpful to you.**

- **If you could change one thing about today that would have enhanced your learning, what would that be?**

- **What is something that you wished you had done differently to enhance your learning?**

- **What other topics should we consider for future meetings?**

- **What feedback would you like me to have about your experience today? Please give examples. Presenters are learners too, and you won't hurt my feelings. I respect your input.**

- **Please give an example of one concrete thing you are going to do as a result of this program today.**

Many evaluations are based on a one-to-ten rating scale from worst to best. While this satisfies an easy need to determine value, it does little to determine real value. Many meeting planners are so used to this way of evaluating it is unlikely you'll get them to change easily. Therefore, try two things. First, ask that your questions be added to their form. Second, have an additional form and tell the audience you are pilot-testing the evaluations to see which is more useful, in order to provide feedback to the presenter.

Kevin was at a meeting where one of the physician attendees was rating a previous speaker on a one-to-five scale. Kevin knew the speaker was outstanding, as he had heard him many times before. The doctor gave him a "three" and Kevin inquired about it (worried about his own evaluation no doubt!). "Well," the doctor said, "you are all outstanding. So, with all of you being excellent, that really creates an 'average' so I gave the guy a 'three' because I thought he was just like all of you—terrific!" Now as convoluted as that sounds, it shows the problem with using numerical ratings. We really don't know what a number is for each participant, even if we tell them what number is fair, good, or excellent. When they write more to us, then we have a better idea what they mean.

Feedback is good as long as you focus on the outcomes and not personal popularity.

THREE THINGS TO DO WHEN YOU BOMB

- Remember there is at least one person in every audience who really liked you and your message! Therefore you were not a complete bomb! And if there is one, there are probably quite a few.

- What do you feel went wrong, and what could you have done about it? Often, things are beyond our control. Take responsibility only for those things that are and were under your control.

- Learn from your mistakes. Next time will be much better.

FROM THE PROS

"Let authenticity shine beyond charisma, substance rise above style, and significance transcend success. Your audience will feel it all and reward you for it."

—Nido, business consultant, author, and coach to professional speakers

62

Determine the Next Step

- **It is your responsibility to think beyond this one presentation.**

- **You can effect more lasting impact with a simple strategic phone call.**

- **Get in the habit of handwritten, mailed thank-you notes.**

As good salespeople know, getting the second appointment is as important, many times more important, than getting the first. So too with your speaking. Make sure you have considered what your next step will be with this group, this planner, this boss, and even with yourself.

For example, will you send handwritten thank-you notes as soon as possible to the important people in the audience? (The correct answer here is "yes!") Ensure that you will with a simple technique—write the thank-you note in advance of the talk and prepare a stamped envelope. Imagine you are an administrative assistant, a manager, a vice president, and you have put more than enough time into this meeting. On the very next day, you receive a warm, affirming, friendly, encouraging thank-you note from your speaker. This is very good business and very good *for* business.

COACH'S COMMENTS

Your coach says: Audiences may leave, but they still need to take the next step. Why not include some "next steps" in your presentation? Use examples you recommend or those from previous groups

you have worked with. When you get specific with an audience,
they have a better idea of returning to their responsibilities and doing something different—but only if you suggest it.

Remember the person in charge of the meeting. Could they
use a follow-up call? Plan some questions you could ask, like, "On
a scale of one to ten, how did you think the meeting went? Why?
What did you like the best? What would you do differently?" Consider if they would benefit from your "coaching" them as to the
next time this group meets. Would they benefit from the offer of
future help? You never know what else you will find out with a
simple phone call that will anchor your relationship.

Some presenters give their phone number and e-mail address
with the offer that any audience member can contact them at any
time for follow-up. This helps the audience feel cared about and
gives them an opportunity to learn more. Most will never call you.
Some will, and that will provide them and you with a rich opportunity. Always leave a number behind.

And, finally, what did you learn from this presentation? What
do you know now you didn't know before? About them, about
yourself, about the challenges they talked to you about—what happened before, during, and after your presentation that was new,
better, different? One technique you can use for your presentation
improvement is to set up a small mini-DV camera on a tripod in
the back of the room. Aim it at the front, turn it on, and forget it.
Any amount of your talk that it captures will provide you with
valuable feedback and a next step in your professional and personal development. Just make sure you don't make a big deal out
of it, don't fool with the technology, and don't keep checking it—
just "set it and forget it!"

**What is the next step after your presentation? If nothing else,
every meeting planner deserves a handwritten, mailed
thank-you from you.**

Part X

Never Give Up

63

Every Presentation Counts— Every Time

- **Give 100 percent every time you present.**
- **Every presentation you give is important to an important someone.**
- **Success may not be what you think it is.**

As you become more and more visible, a great presentation can positively impact both your peers and your management and leadership teams. Your presentation skills will become a real and tangible key to your success. This success begins with preparation.

Presenting well always accelerates your career. Preparing well will always accelerate your presentation skills. Begin your preparation the way that professional speakers begin—with the customer who represents the audience. Conduct a thorough interview with the person asking you to present, even if you have given this presentation hundreds of time before.

Your presentation content will only be a part of your success. Real success in presentations is measured by the effectiveness of your connection with the audience. This happens only when you know the audience, why you were selected, and the standard for success set by the person who asked you to present.

Be diligent and proactive when you are asked "casually" to review the business plan, to update the team on the subcommittee's progress, or when you have to "fill in" for someone who is absent. Be vigilant when you are reporting out from a small group during a training exercise. View these scenarios as opportunities to become visible.

Never treat opportunities to present in a casual manner. These are moments in front of other people that capture who you are, what you know, and what you can offer. Your reputation and their perceptions about your capabilities are at stake. Visibility happens when you are aware of what people see from you, what they hear from you, and how they feel when they are with you.

Be wary of corporate meetings held at the home office. The logistics will not be as complicated, and this is a potential danger for you. When the conference room is right around the corner or in the next building, we tend to treat the meeting with less formality than meetings we fly to or the ones held off-site. Treat every meeting you present at as special and important because there is always someone out there for whom it *is* a very special and very important meeting—and they are in your audience.

Be friendly and hospitable to the administrative assistant. Don't forget the people who actually do the nuts-and-bolts work! These "admins" live and die based on detail. Although their boss is the one you need to please, the administrative coordinators are the ones you must help have a painless meeting. While they thrive on details, those are the same details that can make your presentation live or die! A written (not e-mailed) thank-you note to the administrative coordinator is a wise investment.

Administrative assistants wield great influential power. Too often regarded as the invisible, silent workers in an organization, they are frequently not so quiet with their boss. When asked for their input, they are often the most candid on the team. Your relationship with them is critical for your own success.

Stay in constant contact with your meeting planners, especially those who are corporate veterans, who generally prefer over-communication from you as opposed to not enough. When you must fly in, e-mail them your travel itinerary. Let them know that you have arrived. Check for last-minute details.

You must intend to make positive impressions. Try to influence diplomatically how the room is arranged. For groups of less than twenty people, a U shape gives the group a view of everyone else and you, the focus point for your presentation. Avoid sitting around a large conference table. A classroom-style arrangement limits discussion and remains too commonly used. You may have no influence or power here, but try nonetheless.

If your audience is reserved, try switching sides of the room for balance. This might mean you will move from side to side; it might also mean you will rearrange the name tents so that certain attendees are sitting next to others who you have decided will be helpful to the discussion. Don't be afraid to do this.

Connect with your participants upon their arrival. Emphasize first names on participants' name tags and use table name tents. Introduce any new members to the group. Recognize tasks done well. Build community by fully explaining the goals for the meeting. Tell the audience what to think about or look for as you begin the presentation. Thank any contributors. Paraphrase regularly. Listen.

Develop a liking and sensitivity for people in general. Find commonality, and yet encourage differences. Show your confidence and support in your audience by exhibiting a calm presence and acknowledging and encouraging their active participation. This will be difficult with the more challenging audience members, but it will be a critical test of your ability and your professionalism.

When you are encouraging, your audience notices immediately. They become more cooperative and learn more when you genuinely like them. If, however, you like your slides more, or you like your content more, or you like yourself more, they smell it a mile away and you are done for—and so are they. An opportunity is wasted. When you emphasize their importance, they win and you win, too.

Manage your time creatively and appropriately for the format as indicated by your host. Always, always end on time. Never beg for more time, even if you have been given less than you anticipated. Always face unexpected change with flexibility and positive energy.

Remember, it is your career up in front they are looking at. The audience does not care that you were promised sixty minutes and now you have only thirty. They don't care how important your material is if you are cutting into their lunch or break. And they certainly don't care that you were late and you didn't have time to get your computer hooked up.

The audience simply wants you to deliver a memorable experience—that is the definition of success.

64

Every Presentation Is Different Even When It Is the Same

- **No presentation is the same even when it appears to be.**

- **Your audience dictates the difference.**

- **Prepare, prepare, prepare—especially from the inside out.**

There may be times you will be called upon to give the same presentation. Sometimes you will be asked to give the exact same one. Trainers, salespeople, inspirational speakers, community leaders—many of you repeat a meaningful talk to multiple groups. Resist the temptation to think that it will be the same.

Even when the content is the same, your presentation will be different because your audience will be different. This is also true when the audience is the same but some time has passed. They will have had intervening experiences from your prior presentation that will make them different; they will have heard you once before, and now they have new expectations.

Therefore, when you are ready to give the presentation for a second or a third or even a sixteenth time, prepare as you would for any new presentation: What are the three things you most want to communicate? Who is this audience? And what do they need and want for this presentation? Take nothing for granted. Laughs will come in different places. Questions will erupt over different information. Quizzical looks will appear when they didn't before.

Your content does not have to change. In fact, when you are asked to give the same presentation it is likely that the content will be exactly the same, your PowerPoint slides will be the same, or your boss will simply want the same thing—no changes! This presentation will still be different. In the same way that two baseball teams play entirely different games during a double header, so too will you. Sometimes you will hit a home run; sometimes you won't.

Professional speakers attest to the different ways that audiences react to the same speech. They learn from them each time, yet never cease to be surprised. Cyndi's minister gives his sermon three times every morning in the large church she attends. The 8:00 A.M. crowd is always quieter than the 11:30 A.M. one. The 9:30 crowd is most attentive—least sleepy and distracted. Children are in Sunday school and parents are able to concentrate. Every Sunday, he shares the same words three times with three different audiences, and he has a slightly different conversation with each. The conversation is the subtle part of the sermon. It's really not written; it's within.

Remember that a great speech, an effective presentation, a respectful eulogy, or a celebratory wedding toast is an "inside" job—it is all about you in conversation with the audience.

65

When You're Being Coached, Listen and Respond Carefully!

- **Give your coach a break if he or she hasn't read this book!**
- **When your boss requests change, do so.**
- **When push comes to shove, it is up to you and you alone to initiate and maintain change.**

When you are the one being coached, it is unlikely your coach will do as well as this book recommends! Most corporate executives and supervisors have had little training in coaching. They may hedge around the issue or, conversely, abruptly and brusquely give you too much advice. Whatever their style, here is how to handle the feedback they will give you.

Set both of you up for success. Tell your coach clearly what you want from him, what you want him to look for, and what you are working on. This "personal agenda" will help focus his efforts. It also moves him away from any potentially hidden agenda and on to yours: "I am trying to watch the tone of my voice and my ability to ask open-ended questions. As you watch this meeting, would you keep that in mind for feedback?" This request is hard to ignore.

When you receive feedback from the coach, write it down and say "thank you." This keeps you from becoming defensive; it gives the coach the impression you are taking him seriously; and it provides a written record of precisely what was said for your future reference. Don't fight about it. Simply take the ideas in both mentally and in written form.

Develop a plan for implementing the ideas you both want.
Think about how you would do it next time, read, attend training,
and research. Do anything you need to do to change. Remember
that change might not be easy. We had one extremely bright client
who used the word "guys" whenever she spoke. For her generation, that word is fine. For her audience, people fifty years of age
and older, the word "guys" is considered too informal for a professional presentation. Try as she might, it took her one solid
month of awareness and feedback to break the habit.

Resign yourself to the fact that coaching doesn't achieve
change in one or two sessions. Coaching works with time and
practice. A good coach can only be good over the course of watching you change and improve. Situations change. Managers
change. Products change. Teams change. Coaching adapts and
helps at each step of the way.

Let your coach know if something isn't working. Cyndi has
learned to be assertive with her strict Eastern European tennis
coaches. She likes their high standards but had to adapt to their
abrupt interpersonal style. At first, she did everything they asked
without question. But later, as certain hand positions and techniques weren't working, she gathered the nerve to tell them. The
result was, they spent even more time with her, attempting to explain more clearly. A good coach always will.

Affirm your coach. Tell him or her precisely what you liked
about what he said, how he said it, and what it led to. You are
likely to get him to do more of the same next time.

COACH'S COMMENTS

Question: I'd like to ask my manager for a coach to help me, but
I'm afraid she'll see this as a sign of weakness on my part. What do
you think?

Your coach says: Glad you asked! Actually, research shows that
people who ask for help have higher self-esteem than those who
don't. Don't wait for appraisal time to ask. State assertively what
you want to work on. Say you would like to excel at presentations
and you know it would boost your client relationships, management

ability, project team effectiveness, etc. Then say you are committed
to the process, ready to begin immediately, and want to know your
manager's thoughts about it.

**The smallest habits can be the hardest to change,
but the effort is worth it.**

66

Step Up to the Retreat-Planning Challenge!

- **Whenever you can, become involved in the planning process.**

- **Use learning theory and psychology to have a transformational meeting rather than an agenda-packed transactional one.**

- **Especially for retreats, attendees never remember what the presenter said—they remember what they as the attendees thought and what they said.**

Once you have mastered your presentation skills and impressed your bosses with your newfound confidence, you may be called upon for different speaking opportunities like participating in or even planning retreats for your organization. While retreats can present a variety of challenges, they are also a way for you to show off your presentation, problem solving, and organizational skills. Don't shy away from a retreat opportunity. Instead, consider it a "pro-stretch"! Do your pre-work, listen to what your organization's goals are for the retreat, and above all, remain focused on your audience.

If you are planning the retreat, consider this sample agenda for a two-day meeting designed to address leadership concerns about team productivity:

- **Dinner the evening before:** Program them for success. Highlight the good. Give awards to your highest performers. Speak about their successes and the improvements of each and every team. When they return to their rooms, have a small token or gift for them that the hotel has delivered—everyone gets one—a sweatshirt, a T-shirt, something that celebrates working together. Include a note from you, thanking them and previewing the days ahead.

- **Morning (Day 1):** Use healthy fear. Deliver the good news and the bad news in front of everyone (with no malice, just firm and friendly). Speak of the "others" who are customers, the audience, and the world. Speak of your own aspirations for them, your disappointments, fears, and hopes. Talk about perceptions, misperceptions, and mistakes made across the board. Finally, ask for their help, "This is what teams are for. I need your help, and I need it now." Then, in no uncertain terms, outline the strengths, needs, and challenges you see for the team. Be blunt, businesslike, and passionate.

- **Lunch (Day 1):** Assign seating, placing people who don't know each other well at the same table. Give each table a task, like answering "What did we discuss this morning?" Ask them to develop three versions: one for you as their leader, one for their college roommate, and one for a five-year-old. Give out fun prizes for the most creative versions. (This exercise works like magic each and every time. You can do it at lunch or an extended version after lunch. What it allows for is a clarification of the issues. In fact, most groups we have worked with always prefer the explanation for the five-year-old!)

- **Afternoon (Day 1):** Play the psychology card. Break them up into business units and have them address and assess the strengths, needs, and challenges of their particular team. The task is to discuss and create a presentation in response to you and to the audience. Give extra credit for creativity, honesty, and group presentation. You want each team to involve the audience. For this exercise, you want them to look seriously at their business and their teams to formulate a plan about what they will do to get better, to solve problems, and to meet the challenges.

- **Morning (Day 2):** Put them in work teams across the units, mixed up again so that the teams can "cross-pollinate." Their task: Brainstorm and come up with concrete suggestions for each business unit on how to encourage each unit's strengths, overcome their needs, and predict and meet the challenges. Again, have these groups present to the audience in a creative manner that involves everyone.

- **Lunch (Day 2):** Give awards for presentations. Share your response to their ideas and plans, how they fit into your plan of attack, and your newly revised version of their job description. Give them a very well formed message about who they are.

- **Afternoon (Day 2):** Ask for specific commitments from teams. What will each team commit to over the next three, six, and twelve months that will be "different and better" than had been before? Allow time for a discussion about accountability methods. Use this time for listening, coaching, and reacting.

- **Late Afternoon (Day 2):** Lead through example. Close the retreat by speaking of the process and the results of this meeting, the importance of speaking openly, offering reactions without holding back, and always emphasizing what can happen.

COACH'S COMMENTS

Question: Well, it's my turn to plan the department retreat. What are some key things that will make my retreat the best?

Your coach says: Retreats are more and more popular because staff has a chance to do two important things: work in a relaxed and different culture and accomplish important business goals that are not available in our normal business environment. Make it as easy for them as possible to enjoy this change of culture. Allow "hang-out" and "hang loose" opportunities in every format you can think of. Offer experiences like cooking or scavenger hunts or hiking. Offer discussions with no right or wrong answers. Bring teams together. Make teams meet other teams. Take lots of flipcharts, markers, and gadgets to play with. Have a fireside sing-along or a "come as you are" night. Blend learning with relaxation. Have masseurs and volleyball courts available.

The key is to make it different and meaningful. Another important feature is the business purpose for the retreat. Every event, although fun, should have a business purpose that you can articulate, that the participants can easily understand, and that your boss can justify when questioned.

Retreats can take many forms. Unfortunately, they often take the same form over and over again, trying to get too much done in too short a time. Use learning theory and psychology to have a transformational meeting rather than an agenda-packed transactional one. Transactional meetings are meetings where the meeting takes place, but nothing of substance really happens. These meetings are filled with updates, reviews, mini-presentations of groups, etc. Much of this information could have happened by e-mail or in other written forms. Transformational meetings are meetings where the attendees go away energized and enthused about their organization's initiatives and pledge to work creatively toward those goals.

**Strive for transformation and inject
your creativity for your next retreat.**

THREE WAYS TO ORGANIZE A RETREAT

Retreats and days away from the routine of the office can be extremely valuable if you do three things: involve, welcome, and accomplish.

- **Involve everyone early in the process so they can voice their wishes.** Have a committee in charge of decorations, objectives, activities, venue, etc. Have only those committees that you want to get input from. If you and your boss want to control the agenda and activities, make sure you don't give that away to a group. Decorations, recreation, food, and other amenities are good ways to involve others.

- **Welcome everyone with clear directions, objectives, dress recommendations, hosts and hostesses, and**

a special welcome "kit" that has the agenda, a water bottle, etc. Give them the inner opportunity to say to themselves, "Wow, this is nice! Planned, fun, I'm here, and I'm glad." If your retreat involves a golf outing, leave the organizing to the professionals at the course. Make sure those who are nongolfers are reassured that their inexperience won't cause a problem and there will be no embarrassing moments. If you are planning a specific activity, make sure there are alternative activities for everyone.

- **Make sure you accomplish a business purpose.** You'd be surprised how many employees don't like these days away! When they see it accomplishes a goal, they are much more committed to anything you have planned. It never hurts to do at least one thing that is different. One executive brought in an etiquette expert for dinner. Another time he had a marketing expert come in, and the small groups went on a "scavenger hunt" in downtown Chicago to look for "branding" examples. Still another time, he hired a comedy troupe to teach "the art of improvisation" to his team. Each time this team went away, the buzz began weeks in advance, "What is Ken going to do this time?"

67

Go Forward with Follow-up

- **Design a consultative plan.**
- **Truly successful presenters follow up forever.**
- **Use your expertise.**
- **Assume they need your input—because they do!**

The six months or so following a successful meeting can prove as vital as what went on during the meeting. Self-evaluate and ask yourself: What needs to be most different when six months have elapsed? What will I notice? What will the managers, staff, and my client notice? What are my highest priorities? Who needs me the most? How and when do I need to step outside my comfort zone? Perhaps most important, what have I noticed that has been better or different in the past six months that I most want to be aware of and keep in place?

Become a roving reporter and sleuth. Observe and ask around. Ask people honestly, "What have you used? How have things changed? What still persists that you most want to change? What element of the presentation is helping you do your job the best?" If answers are disappointing or negative, don't get defensive. Ask how you could improve next time.

Take some time and briefly write up the changes you'd like to see—in fewer than three pages—then put them away for a week and do it again without looking. Compare the two versions and complete the final write-up. You are of even more value to the meeting planner and to your boss if you are the initiator of these questions, and it will help you be involved in any follow-up. It is very normal to detect the "where am I headed?" question. Think of it as a hunger pang. It is not starvation.

**Presenters must often lead themselves first
in order to lead others.**

COACH'S COMMENTS

Your coach says: Any sales professional will tell you just how difficult follow-up really is. What can at first seem like a small thing—picking up the phone—often looms large for even seasoned professionals.

What is happening is a combination of fear and courage—opposite sides of the same coin. Part of the psychology of this fear is based on the possibility of rejection—few of us want that! It takes courage to go beyond our fears and take a definitive step that leads us to another place. What many choose instead is to do nothing, to wait, or to react.

The harder task, and the one the client really needs, is for us to take the initiative. Whether we have spoken to an in-house group at our corporation or to our professional association or even at our eight-year-old's soccer awards ceremony, there is always room for follow-up.

Follow-up does not mean you are always looking for more work. Follow-up means you are concerned enough with those you did speak to that you want to extend their learning, their skills, and your influence with them.

Consider doing one of the following as you put together a thoughtful follow-up plan:

- E-mail a short note with an invitation to talk about an "idea" you had after the last meeting. (Do not tell them what the idea is in this e-mail.)

- Drop by attendees' offices casually and ask them what they have noticed about the last meeting, especially what they have noticed that resulted from the last meeting. (Do not give your own reaction first—listen, first and always.)

- Phone attendees with a general idea that you "had in mind" today and request a meeting. (Not too much detail over the phone—you won't be able to track their nonverbal reactions.)

- When you see a colleague in the cafeteria, while shopping with your family, or at a dinner, use the opportunity to plant the seed of your idea with them. (Again, avoid too much detail. Just a teaser sentence or two that will give you an initiation for more is enough.)

- Never sell your idea too hard. This must always come across as a service, as a follow-up thought, or as a concern. (It is even better if you really see it as concern for them, rather than a concern for you!)

68

When You Are Asked, Always Do More

- **Know how to say "yes."**
- **Every time you speak, you are presenting.**
- **Every presentation is either a chance to move forward, backward, or to stay in place.**

When you become known as a good presenter, you will be asked to do many things beyond the normal speech, presentation, report, or retreat. You will become your boss's favorite stand-in and "pinch hitter." Say "yes" to these opportunities, but don't let the flattery go to your head. Treat each and every opportunity simply as that—an opportunity to do an excellent job for whoever asked you.

It is easy to let success go to your head. Real professionals know they must, every time, do what brought them to their success. Yo-Yo Ma, the world-famous cellist, still practices daily in excess of four hours. Gifted actors not only know their lines, they know the other actors' lines also! Athletes train continually. As you work toward earning the trust of those in front of you and those around you, make sure you plan to earn that trust each day.

Never treat a monthly update as simply that. It is more. It is a presentation that profiles you and your team. Make sure you thank but not "over-thank" those involved. Continue by outlining the objectives of this update in clear and concise language. And then do what you do with every audience—remind yourself, "What does this audience want from me?" Speak from their perspective, address the benefits they will incur, and mention not only what you will do for them, but what they will receive from this plan, product, or service. They are your audience.

Ten minutes on a conference call is never that. It, too, is much more. You will have only your voice to connect with the many you cannot see. As a result, they will know you simply by the sound of your voice and the wisdom of your words. As you report, stand with your phone or headset, work from notes, use your hands to express yourself, and vary the pitch of your voice in the same way you do for a presentation. Smile, and if you have a mirror, check your smile. It makes a huge difference on the receiving end. Avoid multitasking. Close your door, don't read your e-mail, focus on the phone, and take notes. Summarize often or at strategic intervals (especially at the end of the call), even when you are not presenting. Always be someone others want to hear from. Yes, they are your audience.

When you are asked to "say a few words" at social occasions, remember to be prepared in advance for the possibility. It matters little whether it is a going-away party for a staff member in the cafeteria, a soccer award dinner, wedding, or a wake. Be prepared to say something even if the possibility is remote that you'll be called upon to say anything. Kevin constantly rehearses, rarely being called on! Cyndi listens and jots down notes, in case she's asked to comment. Both do pretend-speech practicing; they are ready and they want to look and sound professional. Some treat these occasions with a light touch even when they know they have to speak. Don't make that mistake. Those who hear you deserve your very best. They, too, are your audience.

COACH'S COMMENTS

Question: I'm not an outgoing person. What are some ways I can do more? Should I just wait to be asked?

Your coach says: Actually, it's best not to wait to be asked, but to do more as a habit and a personal style. I am always impressed and amazed with those who, in any profession, do just a little bit more. It distinguishes them from their colleagues and their competition, and it makes them truly irreplaceable. You can do this also.

One presenter routinely puts small toys on the tables of the participants. Mostly they are unusual toys, some handmade, acquired on her journeys around the world; some are funny; and all are "touchable" and fun. She starts her presentation by saying: "The toys are for you to play with when your mind is wandering during my talk. It's OK to do that because I know many of you multitask anyway—and I know you are good wanderers, also! We all learn in different ways. The toys will help some of you learn something very new today." Then she presents.

Another presenter always sends handwritten thank-you notes, still another sends a follow-up e-mail, and one I know sends gift cards to a person's favorite coffee spot. Driving someone to and from the airport or showing them some interesting spots to eat or visit in your town are extras that mean a lot. A little extra touch is always remembered.

Important phone calls should never be spontaneous or reactive. Prepare with notes on a card to keep you on track. Take notes when the other person is speaking and use directly quoted words to show that you are unmistakably attentive. Summarize what they want, what you will do, and what you both expect. America Online (www.aol.com) has customer service chatter for every representative. They thank you for calling, they repeat their name, ask for permission to use your first name, find out the problem, assure you they can help you, obtain necessary details, give you a callback number "just in case" of a disconnect, and then they summarize your entire phone call. This is called "clarity," and it is hard to fault them when they are being so clear. They acknowledge repeatedly that you are their audience. Amazon.com is also very audience-aware; they remind you of your buying habits and they don't forget you.

The same goes for your e-mails—especially business e-mails. E-mail is for business development and impression management. There is no room in e-mails for emotion unless it is an honoring one. If you are angry, file it in the draft folder and leave it there. Write your e-mail and then don't send it. Reread it out loud. Rework it carefully to fill in details. Keep it short but complete. Remember e-mail recipients, you and I included, ask two questions when we receive an e-mail—what is this and what does it have to do with me? If we don't get an answer within the first two to four lines of text, we delete or skip over it. When we do get an answer, we respond. This is also true of audiences, except there you will get an entire four minutes before they decide if you are worth it!

Never walk into a meeting again without a clear understanding of the three things you want on the table for discussion. Remember to find the right time, the right place, and the right way. Always look at it as the other sees it—the same way you think about your audiences.

From now on, consider every encounter a presentation.

69

Final Thoughts from Your Biggest Fans

Dear Reader,

Every professional speaker I know has a "signature story." This is usually the part of their presentation that is highly personal, usually funny or motivational, and unique to them.

Sometimes, they weave their signature story throughout their presentation, often at the very end, but sometimes it works as their opener. Once you have heard a great signature story, you become like a child and want to hear it again and again. And, like children, if the speaker dares change but a single word, you will demand it is told the same way each and every time.

Just like we have certain expectations for a Jimmy Durante episode ending, Johnny Carson's opening theme music, the TV shows of *Cheers*, *M*A*S*H*, or *Friends*, we want some sameness in our lives. When the familiar begins, we want it the same!

Both Cyndi and I have our signature stories. Come to enough of our presentations and you will be able to lip-synch them with us!

I would like, though, to direct your attention to another "signature." The one we affectionately call your "John Hancock." A handwritten signature is something you and I sign and see each and every day. It is unique to us. It is our mark. It can be our identity at the bank, when we buy our home, when we say "yes" on a contract. Our signature is our guarantee.

Although our signature changes over the course of our schooling, once we are adults, it tends to stay the same. We no longer experiment with it. It becomes us.

As I bid you adieu and until the next time we meet on some future page, I ask that you look at your real signature as the real story of you as a presenter—who you are to yourself, the guarantee of your best each time, and the irreplaceability of you for your audience.

You will create your own signature story. You will create many of them. Like your real signature, they will do your best work for you when by hearing them others will know who you are, what you are saying, and your guarantee for them.

That is when you'll receive a standing ovation each and every time in the minds, hearts, and even, occasionally, in the feet of your audiences!

Better, you too will hear that signature, and you will rise in self-encouragement for another presentation well done.

My best to you always and in "all ways."

Kevin E. O'Connor, CSP
Long Grove, IL

Dear Reader,

I am honored you have read this book and therefore have been unavoidably "pro-stretched." You have set yourself up for success. I hope you've conquered a fear or two by committing to this process. As I've been writing this book with Kevin, I've been working on some personal stretches, too. Both began with fears of mine.

One is a fear of dogs. Last summer, I had a moment of insanity while jogging along the Chicago lakefront, and decided to agree to a dog for my family. My teenagers had almost given up (I wasn't so sure I'd be a great "dog Mom"). But last summer, an adorable, goofy, yellow Labrador retriever, Max Maxey, entered our lives. As I write this, Max is resting comfortably, dreaming of mallards. Was every moment training Max easy? No! Is it easy now? No! Do I regret having him? Definitely not! As a friend of mine so aptly stated, "Dogs add to life."

The other is a fear of (or perhaps a laziness at) getting better at tennis. I've played badly since college so I decided to take a class at a local park district. They say some paths are meant to cross. Thankfully, classmate Molly Zimmer's crossed mine. She encouraged me to join a women's league. I ended up winning the Level One Championship. But, like all pro-stretching, the story doesn't end there.

In a class after the championship, my strict Romanian instructor, Ille, told me I had to get better—that my volley was "terrible," and my forehand and backhand looked like a beginner's. I admit my pride was hurt, but after a long self-talk, I signed up for one-on-one coaching. I found out I was doing all my strokes the way they were taught twenty years ago! A good coach tells you the truth.

None of us is ever without opportunity to change and grow. I am in midlife, but these additions to my life make me feel young. Sometimes they're frustrating, overwhelming, and hurtful; other times they're rewarding, stimulating, and delightful. Presenting is the same way.

With much admiration and continued encouragement,

Cyndi Maxey

Cyndi Maxey, CSP
Chicago, IL

THREE CLASSIC TIPS, MODIFIED BY CYNDI AND KEVIN

- Tell 'em the news you'll tell 'em like nobody else will.

- Tell 'em like nobody else will.

- Tell 'em the news you just told them like nobody else did.